Digital Education and Learning

Series Editors
Michael Thomas
University of Central Lancashire
Preston, UK

John Palfrey
Phillips Academy
Andover, MA, USA

Mark Warschauer
University of California
Irvine, USA

Much has been written during the first decade of the new millennium about the potential of digital technologies to produce a transformation of education. Digital technologies are portrayed as tools that will enhance learner collaboration and motivation and develop new multimodal literacy skills. Accompanying this has been the move from understanding literacy on the cognitive level to an appreciation of the sociocultural forces shaping learner development. Responding to these claims, the Digital Education and Learning Series explores the pedagogical potential and realities of digital technologies in a wide range of disciplinary contexts across the educational spectrum both in and outside of class. Focusing on local and global perspectives, the series responds to the shifting landscape of education, the way digital technologies are being used in different educational and cultural contexts, and examines the differences that lie behind the generalizations of the digital age. Incorporating cutting edge volumes with theoretical perspectives and case studies (single authored and edited collections), the series provides an accessible and valuable resource for academic researchers, teacher trainers, administrators and students interested in interdisciplinary studies of education and new and emerging technologies.

More information about this series at
http://www.palgrave.com/gp/series/14952

Jon McKenzie

Transmedia Knowledge for Liberal Arts and Community Engagement

A StudioLab Manifesto

Jon McKenzie
English
Cornell University
Ithaca, NY, USA

Digital Education and Learning
ISBN 978-3-030-20573-7   ISBN 978-3-030-20574-4   (eBook)
https://doi.org/10.1007/978-3-030-20574-4

© The Editor(s) (if applicable) and The Author(s), under exclusive licence to Springer Nature Switzerland AG 2019
This work is subject to copyright. All rights are solely and exclusively licensed by the Publisher, whether the whole or part of the material is concerned, specifically the rights of translation, reprinting, reuse of illustrations, recitation, broadcasting, reproduction on microfilms or in any other physical way, and transmission or information storage and retrieval, electronic adaptation, computer software, or by similar or dissimilar methodology now known or hereafter developed.
The use of general descriptive names, registered names, trademarks, service marks, etc. in this publication does not imply, even in the absence of a specific statement, that such names are exempt from the relevant protective laws and regulations and therefore free for general use.
The publisher, the authors and the editors are safe to assume that the advice and information in this book are believed to be true and accurate at the date of publication. Neither the publisher nor the authors or the editors give a warranty, express or implied, with respect to the material contained herein or for any errors or omissions that may have been made. The publisher remains neutral with regard to jurisdictional claims in published maps and institutional affiliations.

Cover illustration: © Melisa Hasan

This Palgrave Pivot imprint is published by the registered company Springer Nature Switzerland AG
The registered company address is: Gewerbestrasse 11, 6330 Cham, Switzerland

For Eli and Joe and kids of all ages.

Fig. 1 Teaching the unteachable. 2016. (Digital image by author)

PREFACE

This book was written as a manifesto, so why a preface? To set the table, situate the project, and lay out the backstories.

The crisis of the liberal arts and higher education has been widely debated in academic writing and public media, and while all writers and commentators define the situation differently and propose contrasting solutions, a broad consensus points to several underlying causes of the contemporary crisis: loss of public funding, neoliberal corporatization, instrumentalization of knowledge, changing demographics, and disruptive technologies. American studies scholar Christopher Newfield analyzes the economic and political offensive on public universities in *Unmaking the Public University: The Forty-Year Assault on the Middle Class*, arguing persuasively that conservative politicians and media have used the culture wars to effectively reduce public support and funding for higher education by attacking its post-1960s affirmation of social equality and diversity. We step back to situate the crisis within a broader historical frame: the nested contexts of neoliberalism, the end of the Cold War, the closing of modern disciplinarity, and the displacement of literate, logocentric knowledge.

At stake in the contemporary crisis are fundamental Western understandings of knowledge and its role in society. Journalist Fareed Zakaria counters politicians' demands for a more vocationally oriented university, arguing in *Liberal Arts at the Brink, In Defense of a Liberal Education* that the liberal arts tradition of analytical thinking and clear writing produces the skills students need in contemporary society. Writing and critical thinking are indeed defining traits of the classical and modern academies, yet we believe media making and critical design are also necessary for the creativity,

vii

viii PREFACE

storytelling, design skills, and continual learning that Zakaria champions. Traditional thinking and writing practices must be reinscribed within an emerging digital apparatus comprised of new sociotechnical processes of identity formation, collective action, and ontological world building. In *Beyond the University: Why Liberal Education Matters*, Michael S. Roth identifies different strands of liberal education: skeptical inquiry, canonical reverence, and social utility—all of which seek to produce a self-situated in the world. Like Roth, we see the solution as moving beyond the university, though we focus both on individual students and collaborative teams as agents of knowledge production and community engagement, self-transformation and world building. 'Figurally' speaking, Rodin's *The Thinker* joins a band, performs on YouTube, and goes viral with articles, podcast, info comics, and PechaKucha talks. More than half of American school children study and collaborate in Google Classroom, writing and creating presentations, sharing documents, and communicating via email. Is higher education ready for them?

We call this emerging onto-historical apparatus *digitality*, a term coined by Nicolas Negroponte to describe as the condition of being digital and which we specify as the global reinscription of oral, literate, and numerate archives within networked databases and computers, and the accompanying transformation of identity, collectivity, and world-making. Digitality displaces literacy and ideational thinking within a wider media and cognitive space. In *Learning Identities in a Digital Age: Rethinking Creativity, Education and Technology*, Avril Loveless and Ben Williamson argue that digital pedagogy entails not only changes in technologies and practices, but also the emergence of a cybernetic mode of thinking which valorizes networks and connectedness. What is needed is a new image of thought and action. StudioLab's *transmedia knowledge* reinscribes ideas and metaphors within post-literate, transmedia knowledge-making. The path we take has been staked out by Gregory L. Ulmer in *Internet Invention: From Literacy to Electracy*. Ulmer's 'electracy' informs our theory of digitality as the electronic displacement of literate thought and action. Scholars working in digital learning describe the effects of digitality in different ways. In *Disruptive Technology Enhanced Learning: The Use and Misuse of Digital Technologies in Higher Education*, Michael Flavin argues for focusing on technological practices rather than technologies per se. Flavin analyzes such disruptive trends as the Google search engine, communities of practice, and MOOCs, and calls for universities to embrace such disruptions more systematically. Flavin's text complements our book: his study

PREFACE ix

of technological practices is itself largely theoretical and descriptive, while StudioLab sets forth a theoretically informed and systematically applied practice based on transmedia knowledge, collaborative platforms, and community engagement.

The StudioLab pedagogy builds on the critical thinking skills students develop in introductory and advanced writing courses, as well as their own course of study. It thus also complements extensive and ongoing work in the field of multimodal composition. As demonstrated in Cynthia L. Selfe's collection *Multimodal Composition: Resources for Teachers*, researchers in writing and composition studies have been developing media projects and assignments for decades. Significantly, in their book *On Multimodality: New Media in Composition Studies*, Jonathan Alexander and Jacqueline Rhodes argue that digital media opens up rhetorical possibilities far beyond those of writing and offer case studies that demonstrate these possibilities. Similarly, in *Toward a Composition Made Whole*, Jody Shipka argues against the limits of the terms 'multimodal,' 'multimedia,' and 'new media' and for a more inclusive approach to the process research of composition. Like others in this field, StudioLab turns to design as well as writing, and we believe that the pedagogy offers a robust framework and language alongside other approaches to working in digital media. Our goal is to reinscribe critical thinking and the alphabet (itself an audiovisual medium) within a wider frame of critical design and transmedia knowledge. StudioLab's critical design approach combines traditional critical thinking with activist-based tactical media-making and engineering-based design thinking.

For cultural, organizational, and technological reasons, the most daunting challenges of developing a robust framework and language for transmedia knowledge production come at the level of research. It is here that the apparatuses of literacy and digitality come into increasing tension, as the print-based models of traditional knowledge production now limit higher education's missions of research, learning, and public service. James Somer explores the limits of traditional scholarly media in his *Atlantic* article, *The Scientific Article Is Dead*, arguing that the fixity of print and PDF files cannot capture the dynamic systems of the world—and of advanced research. In contrast, Somer points to Wolfram Mathematica, a proprietary interactive 'notebook' with text, dynamic charts and formulae, video, and audio. Focusing on developments in the humanities and social sciences, the Scholarly Communications Institute reports in its *Emerging Genres in Scholarly Communication* paper that the relation between authors, readers, publishers, and archives has dramatically shifted

x PREFACE

toward the end users of knowledge, who have become more active and less passive. In our terms, they are becoming maker. Despite increasing recognition of the limits of traditional genres, our disciplines and institutions remain bound to articles, even as the ecology of knowledge production has changed.

The future of the liberal arts may well depend on designing more collaborative and engaged forms of research across all fields. In addition to new genres, transmedia knowledge supports new kinds of arguments (adding abductive leaps and conductive flashes to inductive and deductive steps), new sorts of evidence (multimedia, dynamic, interactive), new audiences (not just specialists, but also communities, policymakers, general public), and new affordances (e.g., not just communication but production and co-production of knowledge across the campus/community divide). StudioLab's critical design frames and its focus on transmedia knowledge embrace both traditional and emerging scholarly genres: articles, conference presentations, and posters, as well as info comics, TED talks, and installations. In doing so, it brings specialized knowledge into a new relation with common knowledge and offers a new image of collective thought-action.

Ithaca, NY, USA   Jon McKenzie

ACKNOWLEDGMENTS

This, then, will have been a book, one researched and rehearsed over 20-odd years of practice, dating back to early StudioLab courses at New York University during the dot-com era and continuing today at Cornell. This applied research has appeared in articles, presentations, interviews, videos, and podcast, informed a successful certificate program and consultancy for students, and generated workshops for researchers in different fields around the world. At the core of this theoretical praxis has been this question: what to *make* of media and performance, thinking and activism? The answers my students and I have come up with have surprised us: *role-play as critical design teams?* I start by affirming the crucial input students and workshop participants have had on StudioLab: this book is written both for and from them. Except for these acknowledgments, it is broadly composed in the second person plural: *we*. In the beginning, I speak for myself to thank others.

I have developed StudioLab working across different disciplines at colleges and universities with different orientations and resources, helping students and later consultants and faculty work conceptually with digital media. Their work has ranged from science to art to engineering, activism to business to non-profit. StudioLab's focus has evolved from making electronic performances to commercial media to interactive knowledge installations to interfaces of everyday life to smart media to transmedia knowledge. The colleagues and students, curricula and infrastructures, and administrators and resources at different schools have shaped the pedagogy's evolving practices and its incarnation in theory, courses, classrooms, funding proposals, and, most sustainably, a certificate program and media consultancy services. There are almost too many campuses to thank and certainly too many people to remember to thank them all. I will do my best.

Six campus communities have supported StudioLab's emergence and growth over two decades. In the late 1990s at NYU's Tisch School of the Arts, I shuttled undergraduate theater and graduate performance studies students between studio and lab spaces, and StudioLab emerged there with the support and encouragement of Peggy Phelan, Una Chaudhuri, Diana Taylor, and Arthur Bartow: I thank them for the wonderful opportunity to teach experimental courses and develop a pedagogy tied to my research. At NYU, StudioLab developed the use of bands, guilds, and teams to interweave cultural, technological, and organizational performances and produce electronic performances and interactive knowledge. StudioLab's early website, available in pieces on the Wayback Machine, was built with support from the old NYU Innovation Center. I thank Vincent Doogan, Jeffrey Lane, and Joseph Hargitai. Among the students sufficiently baffled and inspired by these early projects I want to thank Dorita Hannah, Rodrigo Tisi, Clare Croft, Tony Sant, and Louis Scheeder for their feedback and lasting enthusiasm. An interview conducted in these early years of StudioLab appeared with images of student projects in *The Wired Professor: A Guide to Incorporating the World Wide Web in College Instruction* (Anne B. Keating with Joseph Hargitai, New York University, 1999).

Alongside these early courses, I also worked as a graphic designer, writer, and information architect while researching and composing *Perform or Else: From Discipline and Performance* (London: Routledge, 2001). The research there informs StudioLab's three missions to democratize digitality, democratize design, and remix performative values. At the same time, *StudioLab Manifesto* reveals the compositional strategy of *Perform or Else*: for those wondering, Professor Challenger is a thought-action figure, and this book offers a general praxis of performance. The living juxtaposition of performance theory and dot-com media work during the late 1990s was enriching financially, aesthetically, technically, conceptually, and pedagogically. Working freelance for the accounting firm BDO Seidman and then in NYC's Silicon Alley for the tiny firm Creating Media and the large firm Modem Media, I devised an Artaudian-Brechtian perspective on performing as a "creative" alongside programmers and sales reps. This experience informs a guiding interest of StudioLab: how to refunction sociotechnical systems into desiring-machines? I acknowledge that the mashup of art activism and Silicon Alley may unsettle some. From those BDO years in the Paramount Building (now a Trump Tower) overlooking Columbus Circle, I thank Kirk Nicklas and Debbie Lindner for creating a warm marketing department. From my time working downtown for Creating Media and Modem Media, I thank musician Melissa Lang and collage machine programmer Andruid Kerne for inviting me into the world of information architecture, user scenarios, and pitching to Mitsui executives. Creating Media understood the connections between research and living.

Moving to Philadelphia in 1999 to teach at the University of the Arts, I adjusted StudioLab for undergraduate multimedia students preparing for careers as artists and dot-com designers, while connecting experience design to the activist work of Critical Art Ensemble, Guerrilla Girls, and Electronic Disturbance Theater. Teaching in seminar and lab spaces, I developed the CAT and UX design frames for human-centered design and multimedia studio courses. I thank Craig Saper, Chris Garvin, and Laura Zarrow for these opportunities at UArts, as well as an extraordinary group of students who created mind-blowing work even as the dot-com boom went bust before our eyes. UArts' Multimedia program focused on collaboration and revealed to me its complexity. I call out one team, Team Kick Ass, and its leader Jay Smith, inventor of the Viditar for mixing video live playing in a band, founder of Livid Instruments and the Every90Minutes charity for ALS, and also Agent Kilgore in TOYWAR. Rock on. StudioLab's merger of activism and interactivity can be found in the essays "!nt3rh4ckt!v!ty" (*Style* 30.2, 1999) and "Towards a Sociopoetics of Interface Design: etoy, eToys, and TOYWAR" (*Strategies* 14.1, 2001). The latter text first articulates the CAT and UX frames. I thank Steve Kurtz of Critical Art Ensemble and Ricardo Dominguez of EDT/Bang Labs for their conversations and insights over the years.

At Dartmouth College, StudioLab morphed again as I helped English undergraduates create interactive media and large-scale class installations based on literary and cultural texts. One lesson learned at Dartmouth: public displays of student work are demonstrations of interactive knowledge. I thank Peter Travis, Brenda Silver, Mark Williams, and Mary Desjardins for their support and guidance. My student Eric Rhettberg produced an amazing work based on Gertrude Stein's *Tender Buttons* that baffled me. Dartmouth librarians asked me to imagine a general-purpose media studio, a space that could combine different activities: I thank Malcolm Brown for encouraging me to think about building StudioLab institutionally through the library and campus IT. From these years emerged more research on art activism and interactivity: "Hacktivism and Machinic Performance" (*Performance Paradigm* 1: March 2005).

Two years and one young son later, I was teaching activist art and experimental performance to working-class and nontraditional students in traditional, low-tech classrooms at the University of Wisconsin–Milwaukee. I tweaked StudioLab so that it could be taught anywhere, especially as laptops got lighter and faster, freeing us from computer labs. I thank Patrice Petro, Jane Gallop, Dick Blau, and Anne Basting, Brad Lichtenstein, Aims McGuiness, Jasmine Alinder, and Mark Tasmin for their support, along with all my colleagues and students in the Modern Studies program. During this time, I also reflected on the Floridian roots of StudioLab and its debts to University of Florida professors Gregory Ulmer, Robert Ray, and John Leavey in "StudioLab UMBRELLA" (*The Illogic of Sense: The Gregory L. Ulmer Remix* [ed.] Darren Tofts and Lisa Gye. Alt-X Online Network. 2007). I thank them again here.

In 2007, StudioLab's wandering ended for a decade, as I settled in at the University of Wisconsin–Madison and found faculty, librarians, and IT collaborators to build a media-focused Digital Humanities Initiative (DHI). I arrived at Madison seeking to build a media studio for StudioLab and would leave nine years later having radically expanded the pedagogy's form and content while co-creating associated infrastructure, curriculum, and services for digital learning across campus. The UW Library built a media studio in a matter of months, and over three years, DHI won two major internal grants to improve digital literacy, collaboration, and integrative learning. Of all the texts I have composed, none perhaps are as valuable as the two grant proposals for the Madison Initiative for Undergraduates (MIU). The first MIU grant established a multidisciplinary Digital Studies certificate program ($500,000 in annual ongoing funding for four faculty lines and two media studios) that grew to 450 students in three years. The second MIU grant created a campus-wide digital composition center called DesignLab ($225,000 in annual ongoing funding for a consulting space, full-time co-director, and eight teaching assistants across eight departments) that soon was serving nearly 800 students a year. We had created a small world, and my StudioLab students and hundreds of others could work in media studios, get advice from DesignLab, exhibit in the Digital Salon, and earn a Digital Studies certificate.

The people I thank here range from visionary chancellors to collaborative faculty and staff to bright and incredibly hard-working graduate students. Chancellor Biddy Martin persuaded the Wisconsin state legislature to fund $50 million annually through means-tested tuition hikes for the Madison Initiative for Undergraduates, producing 78 new faculty hires and helping 54 existing and new projects, Digital Studies and DesignLab being just two. I thank her for MIU's extraordinary vision and the legislative victory, produced prior to Scott Walker's first election. This unfolding of this history remains to be researched. I also thank her successors, David Ward and Rebecca Blank, for their leadership and support for MIU, along with campus administrators Ken Frazier, Aaron Brower, Gary Sanderfur, Susan Zaske, Julie Underwood, Robin Douthitt, Kathy Christoph, Ed van Gemert, Linda Jorn, and Bruce Maas. Special thanks to the Office for the Vice Provost of Teaching and Learning, the General Library System, the Division of Information Technology, and the College of Letters and Science.

The Madison faculty and staff who supported these efforts are legion, and I thank Michael Bernard-Donals, Greg Downing, Rob Howard, Kristin Eschenfelder, Lew Friedlander, Mark Nelson, Adam Kerne, Susan Bernstein, Gregg Mittman, Michele Hilmes, as well as Sarah McDaniel, Susan Barribeau, Dave Luke, Josh Harder, and Dave LaValley. Thanks too to David Gagnon and John Martin at Field Day Lab. Special thanks to Brad Hughes of the Writing Center. Extra special thanks to Lee Konrad and Jim Muehlenberg: Jim, it started with you.

I directed DesignLab for four years, where we taught the CAT and UX design frames and helped thousands of students make smart media. I thank my co-director Rosemary Bodolay and College Library director Carrie Kruse for their hard work and patience. Most of all I thank the labsters, the DesignLab TAs: Alon Andrew, Dan Banda, Sarah Bennett, Jim Burling, Mark Dhillion, Michael Dimmick, Jessica Frantal, Kevin Gibbons, Dominique Haller, Erica Hess, Jill Hopke, Caitlyn Iverson, T. J. Kalaitzidis, Mark Mederson, Alex Orellana, Brett Rees, Erin Schambureck, Mitch Swartz, and Steel Wagstaff. Thanks also to teaching assistants Fred Gibb, Laura Perry, and Brandee Easter and to project assistants Annette Vee, Paul Zenke, Ben Emmel, and Elizabeth Harris. Special thanks to labsters Katie Schaag and Andrew Sayler for their amazing, inspiring work and for jump-starting the Madison Performance Philosophy Collective.

I give an extra special thanks to Alainya Kavaloski for her extraordinary work as DesignLab consultant, teaching assistant, and project assistant, and for her contributions to this book.

At Madison, StudioLab focused on smart media, emerging scholarly genres used across all disciplines of knowledge. Responding to curricular needs, I also scaled up the pedagogy for lecture courses serving over a hundred students with StudioLab sections run by TAs trained in the CAT and UX design frames. In smaller courses, I soon added the design thinking or DT frame and role-playing as design firms, while connecting UX to the Wisconsin Experience and the history of the Wisconsin Idea. These efforts generated numerous publications in different media, including the articles "Ouisconsin Eidos, Wisconsin Idea, and the Closure of Ideation" (in *Inter Views: Conversations and Crossings in Performance Philosophy*, Routledge, 2017), "Performance and Democratizing Digitality: StudioLab as Critical Design Pedagogy" (in *Performing the Digital: Performance Studies and Performances in Digital Cultures*, Transcript Verlag, 2016), and "Stratification and Diagrammatic Storytelling: An Encounter with 'Under the Dome'" (in *lo Squaderno*: Explorations in Space and Society 37, September 2015); the online project "Smart Media at the University of Wisconsin-Madison" (*Enculturation: A Journal of Rhetoric, Writing and Culture* 15, 2013); the interviews "Philosophical Interruptions and Post-Ideational Genres: Thinking Beyond Literacy" (in *Inter Views in Performance Philosophy* 2017); and the TEDx Talk "DesignLab & the Democratization of Digitality" (YouTube: TEDx UW-Madison, 2016).

The community engagement potential of StudioLab was first revealed to me at Madison by visiting faculty Nancy Breugner and undergraduate McKenna Kohlenberg, whose English senior thesis, "Digital Media and RelationshipBuilding in CommunityBased Youth Programming," informs this book's final chapter. I also thank Katherine Cramer, whose book *The Politics of Resentment: Rural Consciousness in Wisconsin and the Rise of Scott Walker* shapes my thinking as well. Along with filmmaker Michael Moore, Kathy saw Trump coming. Also crucial here was my collaboration with Charles Connelly, Tom Keegan, and Matthew Gilchrist at the University of Iowa on a Global Midwest Mellon proposal, "MidWest Voices, MidWest Visions: Transmedia Storytelling as Civic Discourse." The connection between media, community, and design thinking comes through my collaboration with Dave Francino and Stephanie Norvaisas at Design Concepts and also Dean Soyeon Shin and Dee Warmath in the School of Human Ecology. Special thanks to Michael Shanks at Stanford, and Philip Auslander for touring the d.school with me.

The sixth campus community to shape StudioLab is Cornell University, where since 2016 I teach and serve as Dean's Fellow for Media and Design. Here I have refigured smart media as transmedia knowledge to help faculty and students across campus engage different audiences, working in collaboration with the Office of Engagement Initiatives (OEI) and Engaged Cornell, Cornell Libraries, and the Office of Faculty Development and Diversity. I thank Vice Provosts Judith Appleton, Rebecca Stoltfus, Katherine McComas, and Yael Levitte; Deans Gretchen

Ritter, Ray Jayawardhana, Marilyn Miguel, and Derk Pereboom; and University Librarians Anne Kenney and Gerald R. Beasley. Within OEI, I thank Basil Safi, Gerard Aching, Diane Burton, Anna Bartel, Amanda Wittman, Richard Kiely, Aaron Goldweber, Ashlee McGandy, Mike Bishop, Rochelle Jackson-Smarr, and Wendy Treat. In the Libraries, I thank Bonna Boettcher, Oya Rieger, Camille Andrews, Suzette Newberry, and Eliza Bettinger.

My Cornell workshops have enabled me to share my work with faculty from Anthropology to Zoology, connecting transmedia knowledge to Cornell's mission of research, teaching, and public engagement. I thank the many faculty and instructors who have been a part of these workshops. In particular, I thank the Knowledge Matters fellows, especially Jen Agens, Julie Nucci, and Gretchen Rymarchyk, who took transmedia knowledge and ran with it in their own courses and community engagement. Thanks, too, to Yael Levitte, Lori Sorken, and guest faculty workshop leaders Ric Bonney, Itai Cohen, and Robert Weiss. I also thank John Eckenrode and Janis Whitlock in the Brofenbrenner Center for Translational Research, and Susanne Bruyère and Wendy Gower in the Yang Tan Institute on Employment and Disability for inviting me to share my work. Among the many other faculty who have supported me, I thank Trevor Pinch, Keith Evans Green, Marianne Krasny, and Michael Hoffman, and also thank graduate students Carlos Aguiar, Peter Delnero, Annie Armstrong, and Kristel Joy Yee Mon. I also thank Doug McKee for interviewing me for his Teach Better podcast series ("Mixing Media and Pedagogies Using StudioLab," January 23, 2017).

In my Cornell courses, I have worked with local community partners through the Public Service Center. I thank its Associate Director Amy Somchanhmavong for recognizing the power of transmedia knowledge. At the George Junior Republic School in Freeville, New York, I thank Tom Watts, Karen McLaughlin, Earl Hardy, and the teens in the Poetic Justice poetry clubs, and special thanks to Public Service Scholar Rachel Whalen for helping to create them. At Cornell Community Extension's Urban 4H Program in Ithaca, I thank Romana Cornell and the Karen community teens at Ithaca's Northside Community Center. And most of all, I thank the Cornell and Ithaca College students in my "Media, Design, and Community Engagement," "Experimental Writing and Transmedia Theory," and "Social Activism and Tactical Media Design" courses for connecting their ideas, passions, and media with those of the wider community. In the Department of English, I thank Roger Gilbert, Laura

xviii ACKNOWLEDGMENTS

Brown, Jonathan Culler, Tim Murray, and Paul Sawyer for their support, as well as Karen Kudej and Sara Eddleman for making things happen. Also important for StudioLab's development have been opportunities to create workshops for different sets of researchers. I thank Dariusz Kosiński and Sylwia Fialkiewicz for hosting a week-long seminarlab in smart media at the Grotowski Institute in Wroclaw, Poland. I thank Martin Puchner for making me part of Harvard's Mellon School of Theater and Performance Research; Maaike Bleeker for my experimental theory workshop at the Dutch Theatre Festival in Amsterdam; Gisela Cánepa Koch for my smart media workshop for visual anthropologists at Pontificia Universidad Católica del Perú; Anna Street for the collaborative workshop with artist Ralo Mayer at the Theatre, Performance, Philosophy conference at the Sorbonne University in Paris; Ruth Kassel for the workshop *Thinking beyond the Paper: Exploring Digital Scholarship with Campus and Community Partners* at Siena College near Albany, New York; Sarah Parker Harris for my presentation at NARRTC (National Association of Rehabilitation Research and Training Centers) in Washington, DC; and Janis Whitlock for my workshops at the Cornell Summer Institute in Translational Research in Ithaca. Finally, I want to thank Megan Comfort of the Research Triangle Institute for *her* workshop "Beyond the Peer-Reviewed Article: Making Research Relevant for Community Stakeholders and Policymakers," which introduced me to the work of the Ella Baker Center for Human Rights. The different sets of researchers, disciplines, problems, and stakeholders I have encountered through these workshops have helped reveal the possibilities of transmedia knowledge production and performative transvaluation across fields and institutions.

Writing this book has enabled me to gather StudioLab's 20-year adventure into an argument, story, and set of figures. At Palgrave, I thank series editor Michael Thomas for his excitement about StudioLab and his support of my arguments. I also thank commissioning editor Milana Vernikova and editorial assistant Linda Braus for their patience and guidance. And I thank my copy editor Anny Mokotow for finding things I missed.

Writing books often takes the support of extended families and I thank Caroline Levine for her love, support, and inspiration over many years. I also thank our sons Eli McKenzie and Joe Levine for doing their chores, making music, and being silly. I thank my mother, Ina Jo McKenzie, for her unconditional love, my father, Victor McKenzie, for his laughter beyond the grave, my sister BJ Bennett and brother Wade McKenzie for putting up with me, and my cousin Rebecca Booth Hill for the inner tube ride. Love and thanks to Garcia Pernola Reese for being there.

Special love and thanks to Martha Gill, Michelle Arnold Van Leer, Karin Campbell, Melissa Goldstein, and Charlie Hill. Thanks also to Ralo Mayer and Sean Muir. Smacks to Jeff Schulz, Walter Salas-Humara, Ken Weaver, and Doug Whittle.

Finally, I thank my partner and collaborator, Aneta Stojnić, for bringing thought-action figures to life. It all comes down to taffy.

Ithaca/NYC   Jon McKenzie
February/May 2019

CONTENTS

1	**Wrestling with Plato's Fight Club**	1
	The Academy as Fight Club	2
	Critical Thinking and the Historical Crisis of the Liberal Arts	5
	The Audiovisual Alphabet and the Power of Logos	9
	From Consumers to Makers: Transmedia Knowledge Production	12
	From Makers to Builders: StudioLab as Critical Design Pedagogy	14
	Critical Thinking + Tactical Media + Design Thinking	16
	From Builders to Cosmographers: Critical Design and Critical Performativity	19
	Projects, Exercises, and Design Frames	21
	On the Use and Abuse of This Book	25
	The Adventures of StudioLab	30
	References	32
2	**Becoming Maker: Creating Transmedia Knowledge**	33
	From Consumers to Makers	34
	Critical Design 101: Making Media	35
	Transmedia Knowledge and the Image of Thought	44
	Thought-Action Figures and Media Cascades	46
	Design Frame 1: CAT	48
	Redesigning Silence	50
	Teaching Critical Design Frames	53
	Sleepy CATs in Disciplinary Homes: Why, What, and How	56

xxii CONTENTS

Sparklines and the State of Bliss		60
What Could Be: A Dancing Plato		64
References		65

3 Becoming Builder: Generating Collaborative Platforms   69

From Makers to Builders		70
Critical Design 102: Building Collaboration		72
Teams, Bands, and Guilds		86
Critical Design Teams as Intimate Bureaucracies		89
Design Frame 2: UX		91
Steel, Cage, and Redesigning Silence		96
Evaluating Collaborative Platforms		98
Experiential Architectures and Collective Thought-Action		100
What Could Be: A Thousand Platos		103
References		105

4 Becoming Cosmographer: Co-designing Worlds   109

From Builders to Cosmographers		110
Critical Design 103: How to Do Things with Worlds		112
Community Engagement and Transmedia Knowledge		123
Critical Design Teams in the Field		125
Design Frame 3: Design Thinking		127
Co-consulting and Transmedia Cultural Organizing		133
HCD and Performative Transvaluation		135
Shared Media and the Orchestration of Performances		137
What Could Be: Plato Cosmogram		140
References		143

Index   147

LIST OF FIGURES

Fig. 1.1 Cornell entomologist Michael Hoffmann speaks at the March for Science rally, Ithaca Commons, Ithaca, New York, April 22, 2017. (Photo by author)   1

Fig. 1.2 Proposed reCLAIM Café for Renne's Corner in the Wisconsin Institute for Discovery by the KAMG group, 2016. (Image by Keegan Hasbrook)   25

Fig. 2.1 Still from "Cancer and Developing Countries." Kristel Joy Yee Mon. Video for vlog discussing graduate research in biomedical sciences. Cornell University (2017)   33

Fig. 2.2 Selections from seminar paper, graphic essay, and video, "The{Silence}Project: Some Adventures in Remediation." (Steel Wagstaff 2012)   51

Fig. 2.3 Diagram based on the *Art of Explanation* by Lee LeFever (2012)   58

Fig. 2.4 Table based on *Resonate* by Nancy Duarte (2010)   61

Fig. 2.5 Diagram based on *Resonate* by Nancy Duarte (2010)   62

Fig. 2.6 Diagram based on Duarte (2010) and LeFever (2012)   63

Fig. 3.1 KAMG group presentation of reCLAIM Café by Miranda Curry, Aaron Hathaway, Keegan Hasbrook, and Grace Vriezen. University of Wisconsin–Madison. 2016. (Photo by author)   69

Fig. 3.2 Make a toy experience design exercise. University of Wisconsin–Madison. 2016. (Photo by author)   88

Fig. 4.1 Screen grab from Art of Transformation demo, created in MapTu by researchers in UMBC's Imaging Research Center to visualize interview content and project feedback of Baltimore community members. The University of Maryland–Baltimore County. (Image by IRC)   109

xxiv LIST OF FIGURES

Fig. 4.2 Cornell students Rachel Whalen and Catherine Giese consult with George Junior Republic students on transmediating their poetry. (Photo by author) 134

Fig. 4.3 Media models framework, based on Grosskopf et al. (2010) 138

Fig. 4.4 Still from "Plato in Play-Dough," YouTube video, 2012, Sophie Klomparens, Caleb Klomparens, and Calvin Klomparens 143

CHAPTER 1

Wrestling with Plato's Fight Club

Fig. 1.1 Cornell entomologist Michael Hoffmann speaks at the March for Science rally, Ithaca Commons, Ithaca, New York, April 22, 2017. (Photo by author)

© The Author(s) 2019
J. McKenzie, *Transmedia Knowledge for Liberal Arts and Community Engagement*, Digital Education and Learning,
https://doi.org/10.1007/978-3-030-20574-4_1

THE ACADEMY AS FIGHT CLUB

Recent books tell the story: *Liberal Arts at the Brink, In Defense of a Liberal Education, Crisis in Higher Education: A Plan to Save Small Liberal Arts Colleges in America, Unmaking of the Public University: The Forty-Year Assault on the Middle Class, Beyond the University: Why Liberal Education Matters.*[1] The academy is fighting for its life. For years, the liberal arts and the humanities in particular have been fighting to stress their importance to society. College and university scandals regularly make front-page news, politicians scrutinize and threaten funding—even scientists are marching in the streets (Fig. 1.1)—and anxious parents steer their children away from liberal arts majors. Students and instructors feel this crisis in other ways too, from protests over race, gender, and tuition to policies affecting sanctuary campuses and the closing of departments or entire campuses—all within a widening sense that liberal arts education has lost its way, if not its value.

The academy, of course, has a long history of fighting, starting with Plato's Academy in ancient Athens. Plato, originally named Aristocles after his grandfather, reportedly started his career as a wrestler, and his broad physique earned him the nickname Plato, as *Platon* in Greek meant 'broad'. But the wrestler Plato turned from fighting with his body to fighting with words, and as a philosopher he founded his Academy as a dialectical Fight Club in order to take on a very different competitor: the Homeric rhapsodists whose myths, songs, and dances, he claimed, could only repeat common knowledge or *doxa* and thus not produce true knowledge or *episteme*. A societal battle raged over how best to raise the Athenian youth: whether they should continue their immersion in the Homeric tradition with its myths (*mythos*) and images (*imagos*), or whether they should learn new forms of thinking and discourse, those of ideas (*eidos*) and logic (*logos*), taught by the philosophers.

---

[1] See Victor E Ferrall, *Liberal Arts at the Brink.* Cambridge (MA: Harvard University Press, 2011); Fareed Zakaria, *In Defense of a Liberal Education* (New York: W.W. Norton & Company, 2015); Jeffrey R. Docking, *Crisis in Higher Education: A Plan to Save Small Liberal Arts Colleges in America* (East Lansing, MI: Michigan State University Press, 2015); Newfield, Christopher. *Unmaking the Public University: The Forty-year Assault on the Middle Class* (Cambridge, MA: Harvard University Press, 2008); and Michael S. Roth, *Beyond the University: Why Liberal Education Matters* (New Haven: Yale University Press, 2014).

The fight was thus about media. In *The Republic*, Plato famously excluded the poets from his vision of the ideal city, and his victory over both Homer and the sophists enabled his Academy to shape the forms, practices, and primary audience of education and research for centuries to come. Media other than writing, such as music, dance, and song, would largely become art (*mimesis*) and cease to function as means of knowledge, thereby establishing logocentric (logic-based) writing and speech as the only legitimate media of thought. Today amidst the crisis of the liberal arts, we must grapple with this Platonic tradition, not to overthrow or toss this tradition out of the ring, but to reconfigure it from the bottom up. For centuries, Platonism has transmediated the world into logocentric writing. The time has come to transmediate knowledge in other media for other audiences in addition to scholars. Outdated modes of teaching, learning, and sharing research prevent the liberal arts from fully engaging its contemporary societal challenges and, as importantly, its own students. *StudioLab Manifesto* wrestles with Plato's Fight Club.

StudioLab is a hybrid pedagogy attuned to fundamental transformations in twenty-first-century social institutions and societies, especially at the levels of values, practices, and media. We can sketch some key tensions between traditional and emerging institutional forms and also consider some work-arounds.

Traditional forms and practices	*Emerging forms and practices*
Disciplinary knowledges and interdisciplinary collaboration within the institution	Transdisciplinary knowledges and extra-disciplinary collaboration outside the institution
Separation of seminar, studio, and lab to divide conceptual, aesthetic, and technical learning	Mix of seminar, studio, lab, and field to integrate conceptual, aesthetic, and technical learning
Scholars as solitary Romantic geniuses	Scholars as idiosyncratic collaborators
Values of originality and specialized skill	Values of recombination and multiple skills
Monomedia knowledge production (print)	Transmedia knowledge production
Tutor cultural forms: nineteenth-century essay, novel, painting, classical music, ballet, realist drama	Tutor cultural forms: twentieth-century magazine, film, radio, graphic design, hip hop, performance
Division of high culture and popular culture	Mixing of high cultures and popular cultures
Publication of research for fellow researchers	Publication and sharing of research for fellow researchers, specific communities, policymakers, and general public

4 J. MCKENZIE

The university traditionally organizes knowledge into separate departments with specialized faculty who hold terminal degrees and teach in distinct types of learning environments: studios for art and design, seminars for the humanities and social sciences, and labs for the sciences and engineering. The goal has been to train and produce individual students and scholars based on the model of the Romantic genius, whose originality and virtuosity make them exemplars in their field. In the wake of the Gutenberg revolution, modern knowledge production has been almost entirely monomedia, and the power of alphabetic print is captured in the motto 'publish or perish.' The university typically organizes both media training and study into distinct monomedia, with writing required for everyone, and visual arts, literature, music, dance, and theater divided up and then separated off for tiny populations in art and design schools. In the liberal arts, the privileging of nineteenth-century cultural forms made sense in the twentieth century, as these forms provided the models for contemporary intellectual and cultural movements. Today, however, the continued predominance of nineteenth-century cultural forms helps to maintain and increase the divide between high and popular cultural forms—even though these nineteenth-century forms were once considered popular culture, today, they are seen as high culture. More importantly, this predominance forestalls the emergence of conceptual, aesthetic, technical, and organizational languages and skills to work in contemporary transmedia forms shared with multiple audiences. Needless to say, the tension between high and popular culture is further increased by the continuing dominance of the book and written essay as the privileged media of knowledge production and the marginalization of media genres that speak to non-specialized audiences.

We may seem to be opposing these two sets of forms and practices, but imaginative faculty, students, and administrators have been finding ways to overcome and work around these distinctions by creating more transversal practices and media. Increasingly, federal grants seek projects involving teams of inter- and transdisciplinary research teams, and foundations offer funds to introduce the liberal arts into professional fields. Administrators and faculty also seek out opportunities for team-taught courses providing multiple disciplinary perspectives around a single topic, and students themselves combine and integrate disciplinary knowledges through dual majors and minors that take them across diverse fields. Community-based research and service-learning courses provide opportunities for students to engage their college learning with communities who have different sets of local concerns and knowledges. And both scholars and communities have begun working in media forms such as TED Talks, PechaKuchas, podcasts, blogs, and info comics. Yet despite these encouraging developments across many disciplines, the liberal arts and higher education in general lack a coherent and accessible digital pedagogy that can be used by potentially any field or department.

CRITICAL THINKING AND THE HISTORICAL CRISIS OF THE LIBERAL ARTS

If one is willing to enter the contemporary educational battle, it helps to know more about the history and terrain of the crisis affecting Plato's Fight Club today. The critical thinking at the basis of first-year writing in universities and colleges remains crucially important at this historical moment when democratic institutions and practices of civil discourse have weakened and come under threat. In a time marked by 'fake news' and 'post-truth,' critical thinking becomes both more necessary and yet more insufficient on its own. If arguments alone sufficed, higher education would not be in crisis. In the US, *critical thinking* means using evidence and logic as a guide to decision-making and is considered an Essential Learning Outcome (ELO) by the Association of American Colleges and Universities. These ELOs inform the evaluation and assessment of academic programs across the US, and most entering students are required to take first-year writing courses because educational leaders believe that critical thinking is essential to becoming not only a successful student but also an informed and engaged citizen. Indeed, the StudioLab pedagogy is designed for students to build on their first-year writing courses at any stage in their studies, extending their critical thinking into critical design and digital media. This extension defines StudioLab's approach.

The battle of ideas lies at the heart of modern democracies, and this book argues that traditional critical thinking and academic writing alone are no longer sufficient for entering into public debates or, moreover, for conducting expert research. StudioLab is informed by the critical thinking of structuralism, feminism, psychoanalysis, critical theory, deconstruction, and postcolonialist theory: decades of critiques, built on centuries of critiques stretching back to Kant, all suggest one thing: critiquing media is like praying against science. Words and written arguments alone are not enough.

To critical thinking and writing we must add *critical design* and *digital media*, design and media that move across many forms in order to engage

6   J. MCKENZIE

different audiences and open new avenues for thought and action. In particular, tactical media practices from art activism, along with human-centered design practices from industrial engineering, can reinvigorate critical thinking and introduce *post-ideational thinking*: a type of thinking based across shared media and popular knowledge and not just the phonetic alphabetic and expert knowledge. The Academy created ideas; StudioLab creates thought-action figures: a wrestling Plato, a Fight Club, the music of ELO.

We can better understand the importance of critical design and digital media by placing the crisis of the liberal arts within a nested set of broader historical contexts. Universities around the globe face daunting economic and political pressures to transform themselves—and the liberal arts in particular have suffered criticism, reorganization, and a crisis of identity. Student protests have become common in the US, Latin America, India, and Europe. What historical forces inform this situation? In the US, the current crisis has at least four historical sources, sources that lead from a California tax revolt all the way back to Plato's original Fight Club. Understanding these sources, which resonate around the world, can help us see both the challenges and opportunities before the liberal arts. Nested within one another, each historical source is deep and profound.

1. The most evident contemporary source is public policies associated with *neoliberal, Hayekian (supply-side) economics*, in particular, the crisis in funding for public education, jump-started by the 1978 California tax revolt of Proposition 13. The effects of the statewide tax revolt have spread nationally for decades and continue to affect US public schools and universities through the efforts of organizations such as the American Legislative Exchange Council (ALEC), which supports reducing public funding for education and undermining faculty governance and academic freedom. The recent election of Donald Trump as US President, and his appointments of Betsy DeVos as Secretary of Education and Rick Perry as Secretary of Energy, threaten both public school education and advanced research in unprecedented ways, and attacks on sanctuary campuses offering refuge for immigrants threaten the very culture of higher education. Colleges and universities have responded to these recent developments in various ways: from protests to official proclamations of inclusivity to nuanced policy and program changes designed to engage communities with public scholarship and service learning. This book

argues that in addition to academic writing and expert arguments, popular media forms and digital rhetoric are needed to engage communities, change public opinion, and persuade policymakers of the importance of liberal arts and higher education in general.

2. A broader but less visible source of the contemporary crisis is the *unwinding of the Cold War since 1989*. Cold War funding expanded campuses in the 1950s, 1960s, 1970s, and 1980s, by building and staffing massive research centers that transformed research, teaching, and campus life. Major federal funding for the sciences (e.g., aeronautics, computer science) and the humanities (e.g., Title VI area studies and foreign language programs) began in the 1950s and helped to create America's modern research universities. However, in the decades since the ending of the Cold War, cuts in basic science research and international programs, as well as the 2013 sequestration or withholding of federal funding, have dramatically affected universities' research and teaching missions, and proposed cuts to the NIH (National Institute of Health), EPA (Environmental Protection Agency), and NOAA (National Oceanic and Atmospheric Administration) could dramatically worsen the situation. It is perhaps ironic that research universities that helped the Department of Defense build the Internet's foundational infrastructure, the Advanced Research Project Agency Network (ARPANET), now struggle to integrate digital practices into their learning activities. Yet notably in 1990, just after the Berlin Wall fell, a new hypertext markup language (HTML) began transmediating the command-line interface (CLI) of the emerging Internet (a portmanteau of *interconnected networks*) into the graphic user interfaces (GUIs) that would define the worldwide web (WWW). What the liberal arts need is an image of thought both multimediated and networked.

3. While the Cold War takes us back decades, another source of our contemporary crisis runs back centuries, to the dawn of the Enlightenment and the modern era. From Rene Descartes' renewal of Plato's *eidos* as ideas founded in human subjects, there arose modern philosophy, science, and humanities, all later supported by such grand narratives as national destiny, class revolution, and Enlightened progress. These narratives, grounded in human subjectivity and universal reason, helped to self-legitimate Western knowledge and power for centuries. However, as Jean-François Lyotard argued in his landmark text *The Postmodern Condition: A Report on*

Knowledge, these modern grand narratives began to decline after World War II with the rise of computerized societies.[2] Modern, universalist grand narratives have lost their traction with the general public and with decision-makers, and now colleges and academic departments struggle to articulate strategic visions and justify their work through performance metrics of inputs and outputs, what Lyotard calls *performativity*. For the liberal arts, such strategic visions and quantitative justifications via performativity smack of raw instrumentalism and have been difficult to imagine, much less articulate with any deep enthusiasm, yet Essential Learning Outcomes and the UK's Research Assessment Framework themselves embody our postmodern condition. What is needed are strategies to engage the dominant performative values of technological effectiveness (doing something successfully) and organizational efficiency (doing it sustainably) with performative values of cultural efficacy (doing the right thing in the first place). In a very real sense, we need to learn to argue and story-tell not only with words and images but also with numbers and diagrams, affects and actions. More importantly, we need to do this with audiences beyond ourselves.

4. With the best and worst of intentions, European modernity sought to export its neoclassical ideals and institutions around the world, creating markets, nation-states, and universities. Alongside its revolutions in science, art, and politics, Western civilization's exploitation and destruction of indigenous peoples and cultures, the alarming effects of global climate change, and post-Enlightenment critiques of *eidos* and *logos* have exposed and radically relativized its universalist pretensions to both master and liberate the world. In the contemporary global crisis, relying solely on specialized knowledge may not be the only solution and, indeed, may be part of the problem. In a very real sense, the presumptiveness of expertise and *epistemic* knowledge has been called into question not only by large parts of the global public and many decision-makers but also by some experts and philosophers themselves. What is needed is a much more holistic, inclusive sense of knowledge, something like a *global transmedia wisdom*.

With this set of historical frames, one can better understand how and why the liberal arts and the university have entered a crisis phase, and also

---

[2] Jean-François Lyotard, *The Postmodern Condition* (Minneapolis: The University of Minnesota Press, 1986).

why critical thinking and Plato's Fight Club need to be transformed and transmediated. The relation between *eidos* and *imagos*, *logos* and *mythos*, *episteme* and *doxas* all need to be rethought, *reconfigured*. What if these foundational terms were not opposed? What if ideas and images, argument and story, expert knowledge and common knowledge could be *remixed*, just as DJs and VJs mix sounds and words, beats and images? What if critical thinking could be *redesigned* to make new arguments, use new evidence, and reach new audiences? This is the first mission of StudioLab: *to democratize digitality, just as nineteenth-century public education sought to democratize literacy.* Digitality is to literacy what Platonic literacy was to Homeric orality: a world-altering transformation facilitated by fundamental changes in identity and social formation, cultural production, and communication technology. The digitalization of knowledge and power allows us to overlay the four historical frames that shape the crisis of the liberal arts, and thereby begin to imagine and design a different academy.

THE AUDIOVISUAL ALPHABET AND THE POWER OF *LOGOS*

Wrestling with Plato's Fight Club means wrestling with the medium of its power. Plato's victory over Homer was in large part a media victory, one whose legacy informs today's crisis of the liberal arts. As Eric Havelock argues in his *Preface to Plato*, philosophy begins by stopping the flow of Homeric performance, analyzing the text to extract and gather occurrences of actions and character traits, and then forming generalizations.[3] Most important, it begins by raising the critical question 'what is X?' (i.e., what is bravery, wisdom, justice?) and consequently proposing abstract general concepts or ideas. Plato triumphed over the Homeric tradition by using the phonetic alphabet to stop the music and dance and interrupt the mimetic flow with dialectical questions, and the alphabet has remained the academy's media apparatus or sociotechnical platform for millennia. Now, however, its function as a meta-technology has been displaced by another.

StudioLab argues for a shift in the design and use of alphabetic writing practices that have persisted since the early academy. For decades, books have been epiphenomena of digitality: this book was researched using databases, composed in Microsoft Word, GIMP, and Keynote, transmitted and revised via email, transferred into XML and edited, printed on digital presses, and marketed and distributed via online websites and libraries. Much like the theater director Antonin Artaud, who sought to

---

[3] Erik Havelock, *Preface to Plato* (Cambridge: Harvard University Press, 1963).

reinscribe the dramatic text within a theater of sounds, images, and gestures, we propose creating knowledge in a transmedia space of learning and research. Students and instructors may be so accustomed to alphabetic writing that we often fail to recognize that *it is a medium*, and indeed, *an audiovisual medium*: each graphic letter of the phonetic alphabet corresponds to a small set of sounds whose translation most of us learn to make as small children, first by following the letters with our fingers and saying the sounds out loud, and then later silently internalizing the translation by learning to read the letters 'inside' our heads, moving only our eyes. We are taught to not move our lips—and barely our eyes—so that the translation seems purely abstract, non-material. Reading aloud then appears as an almost magical process—passing our eyes over lines of silent graphic letters and uttering precise sounds as meaningful words—even while the magic gets lost in educational contexts at national scales. As audiovisual medium, the alphabet has shaped not just the ways we communicate but our very image of thought and our methods of knowledge production. Separation of mind and body, knower and known, cause and effect, genus and species: all come bundled within the literate apparatus.

The truth and knowledge born in Classical Greece are not the only things at stake in the crisis of the liberal arts; power and history are at stake as well, for in the modern era, Plato's Fight Club Academy was exported around the world in the eighteenth and nineteenth centuries as a central part of European colonialism. All the terms that end in *-logy* (anthropology, biology, geology, physiology, psychology, sociology, zoology—just to scratch the surface) are intertwined within the platform of alphabetic learning. Phonetic writing functioned as a certain *techno-logos* to build and legitimate disciplinary fields as proper knowledge, as true, epistemic knowledge rather than common opinion. Plato's Fight Club of dialectical argumentation was institutionalized worldwide as universal reason through academies, government and legal systems, and even Neoclassical architecture with its columns and gardens. All helped to vanquish the 'superstitious' images and myths of innumerable indigenous peoples by imposing instead Western ideals in the name of Civilization, Progress, and Enlightenment. Entering History meant entering writing, and the privileging of the alphabet meant excluding or domesticating other media and cultural forms as legitimate forms and methods of knowledge.

While Plato banned poets and artists from the Republic, Aristotle effectively rescued and housed them in a category we today call Aesthetics—an accommodation many find comforting to this day, even though it has historically excluded other media production from constituting proper knowledge. Thus one studies such media and their accompanying sensory experiences as art, and only sporadically has it been valorized as knowledge production in non-art contexts. Traditionally, art has provided models, inspiration, and even methods, but its status as mimesis or mere representation limits its dialectical force. A second domestication has occurred with indigenous practices and systems of thought: they were not banned outright from the academy but assigned special places as 'culture' within anthropology departments and cultural archives, where they could be written about as objects of study, their rituals, images, and myths being analyzed using methods, ideas, and logic. A third domestication has occurred with popular culture, such as comics and graphic novels, games, websites, and YouTube videos. From the traditional perspective of the academy, these and other forms of popular media are, like Homeric epics and indigenous rituals, full of images and myths (i.e., ideologies) and thus best approached—and fought off—as objects of study, using methods, ideas, and logic in fields such as visual culture, cultural studies, and media studies. What all this means from the perspective of this book: these different practices and forms, deprived of their potential as knowledge production, are reduced to objects and regularly translated (interpreted, critiqued, explained) into highly normalized media forms in a single medium: the academic essay and book, written with the alphabet. Platonism transmediates the world into text.

The alphabet is thus a powerful media technology, arguably the most powerful technology ever invented, for its invention helped to structure some of the founding distinctions of Western culture—those between knowledge and opinion, ideas and images, logic and story, and a host of others. This hierarchical model of organizing knowledge still dominates the academy's approach to the world. For this reason, philosopher Jacques Derrida in his manifesto *Of Grammatology* characterized 'logocentrism' or the centrality of Platonic thought and phonetic writing as 'the most original and powerful ethnocentrism, in the process of imposing itself upon the world'.[4] Derrida went on to coin such terms as 'carnophallogocentrism' to describe the nexus of the power relations connecting ethnicity, gender, race, class, and species to *logos* and the Western metaphysics of presence embodied in speech and phonetic writing. But Derrida's alternative, 'generalized writing,' did not propose to overturn phonetic writing but rather

---

[4] Jacques Derrida, *Of Grammatology*, trans. Gayatri Chakravorty Spivak, 1967 (Baltimore: Johns Hopkins University Press, 1976), 3.

reinscribe it within a more general and open space, and also drew on Artaud to theorize this displacement. So too, we seek to revitalize the liberal arts by resituating writing and critical thinking within design and emerging genres of digital scholarship—websites, video essays, theory comics, podcasts, and graphic essays—genres that not only speak to scholars but also engage communities, policymakers, and the general public in more powerful, efficacious ways than the traditional genres of academic essays and books.

Today, amidst the crisis of the liberal arts, a media battle unfolds between the monomedia academy and multimedia popular culture. In college, students may study literature, performance, and digital media, but overwhelmingly, they are assigned to write academic essays about them. Unless students major in the arts, information science, communication, or engineering, many have likely not *made* anything with any media other than the alphabet—or more specifically, they make primarily in Microsoft Word or an analogous word-processing program. StudioLab offers a transmedia, transdisciplinary approach to culture and knowledge production, one that transforms students from consumers to makers and beyond. This approach reaches out across campus to connect the liberal arts to information science, communication, and engineering, and out into the communities and public spaces in order to connect the power of critical thinking and media design to other urgent means and ends. At a time when universities nationwide strive to tell their stories, StudioLab puts transmedia storytelling and knowledge into the hands of students and faculty alike, so that they can better stake their claims.

From Consumers to Makers: Transmedia Knowledge Production

Imagine reversing the engines of logocentric translation, reversing the flow of knowledge and power from alphabetic writing back into the rhythms of Homer, the rituals of indigenous practices, and the media of popular culture. *That's what StudioLab is all about*: learning to translate or *transmediate* knowledge and power across different media forms for different audiences. In particular, transmediating knowledge and power into popular forms of digital media such as video, games, website, comics, and multimedia presentations and installations. In StudioLab, students learn to make new kinds of arguments and use new kinds of evidence within new expressive media forms, forms that connect not just with specialists but with local communities, family and friends, potential employers, and the general public. It means bringing expert knowledge into a different relationship with common knowledge, and the liberal arts into a different relation with communities and the world.

The power of writing has transformed the world as a cognitive catalyst. More than simply communicating thought, writing *generates thought*, or rather, a very specific kind of thought called 'ideation'—thinking in ideas. Plato helped to invent ideas—the forms he called *eidos*, the eternal abstract forms his Fight Club championed against Homeric image-thinking, based on *imagos*. In the *Discourse on Method*, Descartes updated Plato's *eidos* as 'clear and distinct *ideas*' of human subjects.[5] The ideational thought taught in first-year writing seminars—critical thinking—is modernized Fight Club thinking. Arguments consist of fighting with logic and evidence, and critical thinking remains so important that first-year writing is required of nearly all those entering college. In fact, it is virtually the only course required for every college student: everyone trains to write and spar in Plato's Fight Club! And that's a good thing, for the alphabet remains a very powerful media technology. Through StudioLab, students become even better writers by learning to compose in many more media genres.

Media training must include alphabetic writing but not begin and end there, for there are many other ways to engage thoughtfully with different audiences, materials, and media. Laptops and iPhones contain software programs and apps that turn them into cameras, microphones, video-editors, music studios, photo labs, graphic design studios, website platforms, multimedia presentation machines, and a host of social media platforms for publishing and sharing diverse media. If only there were classes, exercises, and projects that regularly called on students to use these common programs and apps in critical and creative ways—and did so not just in media or communication departments but potentially any field of study. StudioLab offers such classes, exercises, and projects. It is one thing to write a paper on contemporary digital culture; it is another to design and make digital media and enter into the cultural battle for higher education and the liberal arts using arguments and evidence drawn from a variety of sources, both expert and common. *In StudioLab, students move from consumers to makers of media—and then become builders of collaborative platforms, and then, cosmographers or co-creators of worlds.*

---

[5] René Descartes, *Discourse on Method* (New York: Liberal Arts Press, 1956).

From Makers to Builders: StudioLab as Critical Design Pedagogy

One may have never thought of oneself as a maker—and certainly not one on a mission to democratize digitality. We can define digitality as the global reinscription of gestural, oral, visual, literate, and numerate archives into the network of computerized databases (the Internet) and the accompanying changes in identity formation, social organization, and ontological worldview (one's sense of being in the world). StudioLab seeks to play a role in digitality analogous to the Academy in literacy: to help students become makers, producers of transmedia knowledge, knowledge based however in bottom-up, common wisdom and multimedia rather than top-down, expert knowledge based on the sole medium of writing.

To democratize digitality, StudioLab has a second mission: *to democratize design, to help make design's mix of conceptual, aesthetic, and technical skills as common as that of writing, and thereby connect critical and creative thinking through collaborative building.* Alongside Writing across Disciplines courses, we need Designing across Disciplines courses or, more simply, formalized transmedia projects within curricula where students regularly collaborate to produce papers, presentations, posters, and other media projects designed for and, if possible, co-designed with multiple stakeholders. What is missing from the liberal arts, and higher education in general, is a formal language for describing and coordinating the different forms and functions of such transmedia knowledge—and for producing this knowledge in scalable, sustainable ways. *Design provides this language and production platform.* The artist Joseph Beuys once said, 'everyone is an artist.' StudioLab says, 'everyone is a designer.'

Taking up the mission of democratizing design, StudioLab teaches not only to make media but also to approach school and other institutions as sociotechnical infrastructures for creating events and resources. *At this level, students become builders of collaborative platforms and shared experiences.* Mixing critical thinking and new media, students work together performing seminar, studio, and lab activities usually dispersed far across campus: seminars unfold in the humanities and social sciences, studio courses in art and design, and lab work in sciences and engineering. StudioLab students can combine these activities in a single space by mixing critical thinking, media-making, and human-centered design in coordinated projects. This collaborative, building dimension is crucial to the pedagogy, for it opens up academic learning to a fourth space: the field of community engagement. It is in this field that transmedia knowledge really thrives, for here expert knowledge meets common knowledge, the liberal arts meet everyday life, and the legacies of literacy and orality merge into digitality.

By combining critical thinking and media design, StudioLab can be understood as a *critical design pedagogy* for democratizing digitality, for inventing and disseminating new forms of post-Platonic thought, and new spaces for action. The term 'critical design' was introduced by interaction designers Anthony Dunne and Fiona Raby to describe design infused with a politically critical sensitivity, both for designer and end user.[6] Human computer interaction (HCI) designers Jeffrey Bardzell and Shaowen Bardzell write that '[b]y inscribing alternative values in designs, critical design cultivates critical attitudes among consumers and designers alike, creating demand for and supporting the professional emergence of alternative design futures.'[7] Bardzell and Bardzell draw upon the schools of Critical Theory and Metacriticism to open up Dunne and Raby's critical design practice for extension into their field of HCI.

In the spirit of democratizing digitality and design, StudioLab likewise seeks to extend a specific mix of critical design across, potentially, all fields. Like performance and media, design is a transdisciplinary and sometimes contested field marked by disciplinary borders and territorial disputes. But when viewed from the perspective of digitality, debates between specialists, as well as tensions between experts and amateurs, can be recast as effects of ideational specialization and institutional habits associated with literate, disciplinary knowledge production. StudioLab's own metacritical move is to affirm such critical differences by devising creative syntheses across diverse bodies, media, and sites, thereby contributing to the emergence of critical design as a creative force for democratizing digitality.

---

[6] Anthony Dunne and Fiona Raby, "Critical Design FAQ," retrieved April 1, 2016, http://www.dunneandraby.co.uk/content/bydandr/13/0.

[7] Jeffrey Bardzell and Shaowen Bardzell, "What Is 'Critical' about Critical Design?" *CHI '13 Proceedings of the SIGCHI Conference on Human Factors in Computing Systems* (New York: ACM, 2013), 3297–3306.

CRITICAL THINKING + TACTICAL MEDIA + DESIGN THINKING

StudioLab's approach to critical design pedagogy combines critical thinking (broader than Critical Theory), design thinking (broader than HCI), and tactical media (broader than writing, as described below). This broadening of scope situates Critical Theory, Metacriticism, and other methodological schools within the larger, disciplinary context of critical thinking in higher education. As noted, critical thinking refers to the use of evidence-based, logical reasoning as a guide to ethical decision-making and action and is considered an Essential Learning Outcome, along with others such as integrative learning, and traditional and digital literacy. The tradition of critical thinking stretches from Socrates to Descartes to Kant to Arendt. It forms the foundation of disciplinary research and liberal arts education and is thus taught across the breadth of the traditional arts and sciences.

From the perspective of digitality, critical thinking is literate, ideational thinking whose disciplinary methods all bring objects clearly and distinctly before subjects, a relationship carefully set up in first-year writing courses at the level of sentences, paragraphs, and essay structure. StudioLab's goal is not to replace critical thinking and writing, but indeed assumes their importance and that students have taken such courses: the goal is precisely to supplement and embed literate methods, subjects, and objects within the emerging digital apparatus, using media and collaborative problem-solving to connect them with new communities and situations. The *logos* of critical thinking and specialized knowledge remains operational, but its efficacy has waned due to the global and historical factors outlined above. Arguments and evidence alone no longer suffice, if they ever truly did. Given the increasingly public crisis of the liberal arts in a period of fake news and post-truth politics, revitalizing the forms, functions, and sites of critical thinking is crucial—but thinking and acting beyond the specialized knowledge of Platonic ideation is also necessary to reimagine higher education's place in the contemporary world. StudioLab starts with three simple steps: first, create transmedia knowledge to connect the expert spaces of seminar, studio, and lab; second, build collaborative projects that share transmedia experiences; and third, connect these experiences out into the common field of community to effect change in the world.

To connect seminar learning with studio activities, the second element of StudioLab's critical design pedagogy is *tactical media*, which emerges out of artist activist events and groups in Europe and North America, such as Next Five Minutes (N5M), Critical Art Ensemble (CAE), and Electronic Disturbance Theater (EDT): 'The term "tactical media" refers to a critical usage and theorization of media practices that draw on all forms of old and new, both lucid and sophisticated media, for achieving a variety of specific noncommercial goals and pushing all kinds of potentially subversive political issues.'[8] Tactical media is critical media that extends practices of civil disobedience into digital culture. In *Digital Resistance*, CAE situates tactical media within a comprehensive set of practices that go beyond street-based resistance against disciplinary institutions to function as digital resistance within our contemporary performative matrix. Tactical media-making enables StudioLab to supplement traditional seminar studies of argumentative and rhetorical writing with studio and lab work that produces a full range of media effects: from the Guerrilla Girls' poster infographics to Reverend Billy's performance protests to Electronic Disturbance Theater's FloodNet software to Molleindustria's absurdist games. Significantly, such media making entails collaborative action rather than the solo efforts modeled on the Romantic genius. StudioLab models its critical design teams on art activist cells, garage bands, and startups: different tutor groups will resonate with different curricular needs and different student bodies.

Supplementing critical thinking and tactical media, the third component of StudioLab's critical design pedagogy is *design thinking*, a human-centered design approach to collaborative problem solving developed by the design firm IDEO and researched and taught by the Hasso Plattner Institutes of Design at Potsdam University, Germany, and Stanford University, USA. Design thinking is an interdisciplinary method for addressing complex organizational and social problems. IDEO's CEO Tim Brown argues that designers must 'think big,' think beyond designing endless objects for meaningless needs and instead tackle complex problems facing individuals and societies, such as healthcare and climate change.[9] Design

---

[8] N5M, cited in Critical Art Ensemble, *Digital Resistance: Explorations in Tactical Media* (New York: Autonomedia, 2001), 5.

[9] Tim Brown, "Designers – Think Big!" (*TED: Ideas Worth Spreading*. Video. September 2009), https://www.ideo.com/news/tim-brown-urges-designers-to-think-big-at-tedglobal.

thinking's interdisciplinary design method balances three constraints—human desirability, economic viability, and technical feasibility—constraints which correspond to the performative values of cultural efficacy, organizational efficiency, and technical effectiveness. Moreover, design thinking's human-centered approach prioritizes human desirability/cultural efficacy, focusing on empathy with various stakeholders to define and reframe the situation at hand. Although design thinking also stresses ideation, or the creative generation of ideas as central to its iterative process, this ideation is post-Platonic, in that relies not on top-down, expert knowledge or *episteme*, but rather on empathizing with a variety of stakeholders, that is, on bottom-up, common knowledge or *doxa*. In that sense, it is already critical, though this criticality resides in a matrix of empathy gathered through ethnographic methods of interview, observation, and participation, and composed of emotions, knowledge, and values. It is within this matrix that micro-transvaluations can occur at both individual and group levels, revalorizations that produce, not exclusions of effectiveness and efficiency, but remixes of them in different, more efficacious spaces.

The elements of StudioLab's critical design pedagogy supplement one another. StudioLab combines the epistemological force of critical thinking's *logos* with the collaborative empathy-driven *doxa* of design thinking and the radical, subversive potential of tactical media-making as *graphe*—not just writing, but drawing, graphics, scenography, animation, data visualization; indeed, any mode of material inscription. At the level of production, traditional critical thinking pedagogies produce individual thinkers and writers, whereas design thinking and tactical media entail the production of *critical design teams*. These teams comprise StudioLab's collaborative dimension. Both design thinking and tactical media-making rely on practice-based collaboration, and design thinking produces its own version of tactical media: the shared media of sketches, diagrams, and prototypes which emerge as part of its design process. Like tactical media, shared media does not report on things but makes things happen: they are themselves performative, not constative, though their actions become reports through iteration. Of course, critical thinking too has its own tactical and shared media: the alphabet, books, and the archive—which most students spend their entire school life learning to the exclusion of other media. StudioLab is a crash course in transmedia critical design.

From Builders to Cosmographers: Critical Design and Critical Performativity

As makers of media and builders of platforms, students can enter the battle over the liberal arts at the level of knowledge-power. The skills they develop by working in critical design teams combine cultural, technological, and organizational performances as well as the values of efficacy, effectiveness, and efficiency. To address the constraints imposed on building alternative platforms, and to affirm the efforts of builders wrestling with these constraints, StudioLab draws on the field of Critical Management Studies (CMS), where researchers have introduced Critical Theory and post-structuralist thought into the discipline of organizational management. Like critical design, critical management studies explore more subversive forms of critical thinking and does so in institutions ruled by socially dominant values and practices; values and practices which its scholars have explicitly theorized in terms of performativity. Again, performativity legitimates knowledge and power by calculating input/output ratios. Whether one feels like a number or embraces excellence, performativity is already at work.

StudioLab offers students different ways to approach performative knowledge and power, and critical management studies offer important lessons. CMS is characterized by 'its critical stance towards institutionalized social and intellectual practices, such as the profit imperative, racial inequality or environmental irresponsibility.'[10] To take on performativity, CMS scholars Wickert and Schaefer invent the concept of *critical performativity*, which offers a nuanced approach as it addresses both the efficiency-effectiveness and efficacy-circuits of power and knowledge. Spicer, Alvesson, and Kärreman further refine the critical performativity concept by contrasting Lyotard's performativity (input/output ratios) and resistant practices of performative speech described by cultural theorist Judith Butler: performativity as subversive resignifications or reuses of discourse—much like DJs remobilize bits of music to produce different effects.

---

[10] Christopher Wickert and Stephan M. Schaefer, "Towards a Progressive Understanding of Performativity in Critical Management Studies," *Human Relations* (2014), 2. DOI: 10.1177/0018726713519279.

20   J. MCKENZIE

Spicer, Alvesson, and Kärreman approach 'performativity as possibly subversive mobilizations and citations of previous performances, instead of as an overarching concern for efficiency,' and argue for understanding and developing critical management studies as a potentially subversive field of performative research.[11] Here critical performativity operates through 'an affirmative stance, an ethic of care, a pragmatic orientation, engagement with potentialities, and striving for a normative orientation,'[12] one that would challenge the reduction of knowledge and power to inputs and outputs. Rather than positioning organizations as objects of critique and researchers as outside performativity, their 'performative CMS' envisions workers as actively involved in liberating performative practices that produce resignifications, heterotopias, and micro-emancipations, practices which CMS researchers should actively engage with through participatory methods. The goal of this critical performativity is 'to not only engage in systematic dismantling of existing managerial approaches, but also try to construct new and hopefully more liberating ways of organizing.'[13]

Critical performativity and performative CMS provide StudioLab with important approaches for combining cultural, organizational, and technological performances within the context of engaging performative knowledge and power. Resignification entails the reuse or refunctioning not only of discourses but also practices and infrastructures and their simultaneous reinscription within newly imagined heterotopias: spaces with alternative conceptual, physical, architectural, digital, environmental, spiritual, and even cosmic dimensions. Indeed, StudioLab functions as a heterotopia for generating heterotopias—a space of difference for creating other spaces of difference across a range of scales. Within this context, micro-emancipations entail not just resignification but more systemic transvaluations of performative values, challenging the dominant circuits of efficiency-effectiveness with those of efficacy. At the same time, making this valorization of efficacy sustainable and scalable depends upon alternative revalorizations of efficiency and effectiveness.

The methods of design thinking and tactical media supplement traditional methods of critical thinking by introducing interventionist media-

---

[11] André Spicer, Mats Alvesson and Dan Kärreman, "Critical performativity: The unfinished business of critical management studies," *Human Relations* 62 (2009): 544.

[12] Ibid., 546.

[13] Ibid., 555.

making and human-centered design. *Beyond isolated critiques of the bad, collaborative creations of joy.* As we will see, these joyful creations can be as simple as transmediating a paper into comics. It may seem counterintuitive to initiate joyful collaborations at the intersection of technological and organizational performance, but as CAE argues, the development of tactical media best occurs within tightly knit groups, teams which depend on a shared generation of ideas and projects, coordinated critical thinking, the organization of diverse talents—and effective project management.

To gather the goals of StudioLab: alongside its missions to democratize digitality and democratize design, StudioLab's third mission is *to remix performative values, to resist global performativity—the legitimation of knowledge and power by input/output matrices—by interjecting values of cultural efficacy into institutions dominated by circuits of organizational efficiency and technical effectiveness.* The call here is to *become cosmographer*: to generate micro- and macro-transvaluations of values that move across visceral, affective, and cognitive realms in order to effect changes within larger systems, and thus, imagine and design new worlds. This is what it means to become cosmographer.

Projects, Exercises, and Design Frames

StudioLab's critical design pedagogy synthesizes traditional critical thinking, interventionist tactical media, and interdisciplinary design thinking by enabling students to combine seminar, studio, and lab activities. *Bodies learn differently in each space.* Students combine cultural, organizational, and technological performances and thereby gain hands-on experience in revalorizing efficacy, efficiency, and effectiveness. At the heart of StudioLab are projects, exercises, and design frames that integrate conceptual, aesthetic, technical, and social learning through individual exercises and larger collaborative projects. In an initial Make a Toy exercise, for instance, students use common household materials to design and create toys—tiny desiring-machines crafted to generate joy in others—while learning principles of experience design, the shaping of interactions, emotions, and thought. Concepts are spatialized, taken back to the drawing board and connected with others, and then explored through hands-on engagement. StudioLab's project-based pedagogy unfolds by juxtaposing studio exercises with seminar discussion, lab training, and time for fieldwork, presentation, and reflection. In another exercise, Design a Museum, students self-organize and scale up their desiring-machines into critical design teams, thereby role-playing as an intimate bureaucracy. By researching art activist groups and miming their different mixes of social activism and tactical media, critical design teams develop names, logos, and mission statements, while drawing on local public commons and transferring their research to issues and situations that resonate with their own lives. Like all StudioLab projects, Design a Museum is modular and portable: it can embrace potentially any topic, field, or community.

As detailed in later chapters, StudioLab's pedagogy moves people transversally in three ways and provides critical design frames at each step. First on a spatial level, within a course, workshop, or even a single, three-hour class meeting, we might begin with a hands-on studio installation, then shift to a seminar discussion, a lab for software training, and conclude with an open workshop or field work. To help articulate these spatial moves with shifts in learning activities, we introduce the CAT design frame (Conceptual-Aesthetic-Technical). CAT maps onto seminar, studio, and lab activities that can unfold in the same space by simply moving tables and chairs. Around a single seminar table, conceptual work follows traditional critical thinking methods—reading, discussion, and written synthesis of textual and other materials—that are supplemented with dramaturgical and media approaches: students generate notes, conceptual spreadsheets visualizing different methods, and intellectual dialogues dramatizing ideational arguments. Shifting furniture into clusters of work tables, aesthetic studio work focuses on transmediating discursive and material practices, mixing arguments with physical, visual, aural, and environmental media, while drawing on fields of performance, graphic design, cinematography, installation, and experience design. Tactical media here include objects, storyboards, mood boards, user scenarios, posters, installations, and prototypes. CAT's technical dimension unfolds in lab formation, with tables now in rows with students learning and using digital software and hardware to support the conceptual and aesthetic activities. Movement between spatial arrangements and their activities are guided by the design process. Generally, projects begin with seminar, then move into lab, and then conceptual and technical work merge in the studio's aesthetic activities. It is important to note that seminar, studio, and lab activities each have their own blends of conceptual, aesthetic, and technical activities, and these come to the fore in different ways. Over time, StudioLab's iterative process blends these dimensions precisely by incorporating their elements into the unfolding project. Students use CAT to analyze, evaluate, and create transmedia knowledge, for it enables them to abstract and evaluate conceptual, aesthetic, and technical issues at any time in the design process. In all cases, at this first level, student minds and bodies are shaped by transversal movement through distinct learning environments: seminar, studio, and lab.

At a second and more intimate level, students build patterns of social and technical interactions: between students and machines, teams and networks, audiences and interfaces. At this level, movement is experiential—*transmedia knowledge moves us.* StudioLab's second design frame, UX or user experience, draws on fields of rhetoric, design, performance, and psychology to explore ways of transforming people internally by moving them spiritually, conceptually, imaginatively, emotionally, sensually, and/or viscerally. Such experiences unfold in schools, museums, churches, community centers, theme parks, everyday life, online or off. StudioLab's UX frame focuses on *experience design* or the crafting of experiential interactions, *information architecture* or the spatiotemporal structure of these experiences, and *information design* or the look-and-feel at any moment of their unfolding. Using the UX frame both analytically and synthetically, students work in teams to build collaborative platforms and shared experiences for multiple stakeholders: community collaborators, target audiences, the general public, and themselves. To this end, teams study how early ACT-UP members transformed their personal anger and fear into love and action by using social activism and tactical media, and creating direct actions designed in turn to transform the feelings, thoughts, and actions of their target audiences and the wider general public. Shared experiences build collaborative platforms. In our Transform a Paper into an App, Service, or Social Movement project, teams scale up their intimate bureaucracies toward sustainable, collective assemblages of enunciation where transformations of larger social systems become possible. At this second level, students use the UX frame to engage internal, 'experiential architectures' of different stakeholders. These experiential architectures form the building blocks of the emerging heterotopias and provide the platform for micro-transvaluations of value.[14]

---

[14] Unlike optimistic utopias and pessimistic dystopias, hetereotopias offer different and sometimes undecidable spaces. See Michel Foucault and Jay Miskowiec, "Of Other Spaces," (*Diacritics* 16: 1, Spring, 1986), 22–27.

At a third, sociotechnical level, StudioLab's critical design pedagogy moves students transversally across different social fields as they connect and engage people across disciplines, institutions, and communities. We draw on a third design frame, design thinking or DT, to tackle intractable 'wicked problems,' by using social activism and tactical media to connect students to community, culture, and history. For instance, in a Museum of Interactive Media project, teams at the University of Wisconsin–Madison researched and proposed activist installations for an underutilized space at the transdisciplinary research center in the Wisconsin Institute for Discovery (WID). The center is built on the former site of Rennebohm's Pharmacy, known for the storytelling of its founder Oscar Rennebohm, who later served as state governor of Wisconsin. Inspired by Reverend Billy's Earthellujah project, the KAMG student design team composed of Miranda Curry, Aaron Hathaway, Keegan Hasbrook, and Grace Vriezen interviewed current and potential WID visitors. They also researched the university's own legacy of environmental research and art activism. Their proposed reCLAIM Cafe offers a post-apocalyptic experience for both reclaiming personal space and measuring one's extension into ecological systems. At the VR Bar, patrons can view impacted environments local and global, download a mobile app to track their waste habits, energy consumption, and water usage. At the same time, Trash Chutes visibly recycle consumer objects all around them (Fig. 1.2).

In StudioLab, ideas function as means rather than ends, entering into an open, iterative process where collaborative problem-solving and creativity unfold via shared media and the posing of counterfactual possibilities within imagined worlds. As teams apply DT's transdisciplinary process of empathy, re/definition, ideation, prototyping, and testing, ideas become collective *thought-action figures*, moving from virtual to actual across different spaces. Most importantly, design thinking explicitly seeks to balance three values: human desirability, technical feasibility, and economic sustainability—corresponding to the performative values of cultural efficacy, technical effectiveness, and organizational efficiency.

Together, the three critical design frames of CAT, UX, and DT, along with associated projects and exercises, provide the concrete means for actualizing StudioLab's mission of democratizing digitality and design, as well as transvaluating performative values. Obviously, a single StudioLab course or workshop offered at isolated institutions cannot alone achieve these missions; it must be part of a larger transformation within the liberal arts.

1 WRESTLING WITH PLATO'S FIGHT CLUB   25

Fig. 1.2 Proposed reCLAIM Café for Renne's Corner in the Wisconsin Institute for Discovery by the KAMG group, 2016. (Image by Keegan Hasbrook)

On the Use and Abuse of This Book

To revitalize the liberal arts, we must transform Plato's Fight Club at the levels of space and media, habits and curricula, values and institutions. Given the social, political, and economic pressures on higher education, we cannot rely solely on expert disciplinary knowledge and traditional media genres of expository essays, journal articles, and academic books, as these speak almost exclusively to specialized scholars. Nor can we keep seminar, studio, and lab learning totally separated from each other and from the field of communities, organizations, and the world. We clearly still need scholars, knowledges, genres, and spaces, but to engage with the general public, with policymakers, with organizations, and with a generation of students raised on iPhones and YouTube and schooled in Google Classroom, we must supplement traditional academic genres with digital media genres such as multimedia presentations, video essays, podcasts, and websites, and bring disciplinary expertise into a new relationship with nonspecialists as well as with our own lives. That is, we must transmediate knowledge and power and create new modes of social contestation and new worlds of cultural imagination. The very life forms defeated or sidelined by Plato's Fight Club—Homeric mimesis, indigenous traditions, popular culture—offer models and mediums for remixing *logos* and *mythos*, *eidos* and *imagos*, *episteme* and *doxa*.

StudioLab can be used in potentially any field interested in generating or sharing research with different audiences. We can appreciate this flexibility through the CAT design frame: the conceptual component can be any disciplinary knowledge; the aesthetic style can range from coherent clarity to sublime subtlety to manic mashup; the technical media can spread from books and zines to videos, podcasts, installations and beyond. The specific mix of conceptual, aesthetic, and technical components will be determined by the particular project at hand and may well be co-created with partners outside the academy. StudioLab's critical design pedagogy combines critical thinking, tactical media, and design thinking in order to bring digital media, analysis, and creativity to collaborative problem-solving and trouble-making.

Even though StudioLab may be used in any department or discipline, its transmedia knowledge forms, design frames, and projects may be more appropriate for some classes than others. If an instructor or department decides to explore the pedagogy, they may want to focus strategically on specific types of courses, including:

- *Entry-level or gateway courses*, thus enabling lower-level students to produce transmedia knowledge throughout their college experience.
- *Upper-level capstone courses*, so that seniors can integrate their learning from their major field and broad liberal arts education in sophisticated, expressive ways, and gather them into a portfolio of work that can be used to take the next step in their lives.

- *Graduate-level courses* to prepare researchers to communicate their work to different audiences and to teach and/or problem-solve effectively in academic and nonacademic careers.
- *Professional development workshops for faculty and research staff,* offering them ways to transmediate their own research and incorporate transmedia knowledge into their teaching.
- *Community-based research, service learning courses, or public humanities and science initiatives* where students can actively collaborate with groups using a transdisciplinary set of critical design skills to address specific real-world issues and problems.

As these courses and workshops suggest, StudioLab can also help departments reimagine their curricular and strategic goals as they wrestle with the crisis of the liberal arts in their own institutional situation.

Depending on the historical context, organizational culture, and technical infrastructure, departments and programs can use StudioLab to *align, transform,* or in some cases *resist* broader institutional initiatives in such areas as program innovation, interdisciplinary research and teaching, active learning, project-based collaboration, community engagement, professional development, technology-enhanced learning, and program assessment. From working across campuses at different types of institutions, we have found that forces of experimentation and normalization can arise and be experienced differently depending on disciplinary field, methodological training, and individual disposition. What seems revolutionary and transformative to some may seem reactionary and soul-killing to others. Some faculty will 'get' StudioLab's critical design missions of democratizing digitality, democratizing design, and transvaluating performative values, while others will not.

Traditionally, undergraduates are initiated into majors and learn objects and fields, but few learn about disciplines. Graduate students are initiated into disciplines and learn methods of research and sometimes teaching, but few learn much about the wider institution. Young faculty are initiated into institutions and learn about resources and funding, but even then, they can remain siloed with little knowledge about infrastructure and community. StudioLab seeks to collapse these divisions and give everyone an opportunity to think and act critically across disciplines, institutions, and communities. Given their distribution requirements, undergraduates are the most radically interdisciplinary scholars on campus, yet they don't know about disciplines, and have very few opportunities to integrate all

28   J. MCKENZIE

the learning gathered while roaming for years across campus. Graduate students and faculty tend to become more and more specialized; though some undertake interdisciplinary research, relatively few problem-solve far from their discipline by using transdisciplinary and community-engaged research. Such specialization may have made sense in the past but today must be supplemented with more holistic and integrated learning.

This book is organized to help design StudioLab courses or projects at any level with any student and potentially any content found in the liberal arts, as well as professional fields such as healthcare, engineering, and business. StudioLab's versatility derives from several factors. First, because it seeks to democratize digitality and critical design within higher education institutions that privilege writing and critical thinking, StudioLab's target audience are college students with little or no prior media design experience beyond first-year writing, whether they are undergraduate or graduate students. Graduate students struggle with design problems as much as undergraduates and take as much joy in creating solutions. Second, because StudioLab focuses on transmedia knowledge, even students specializing in graphic design, video production, communications, information science, computer science, or engineering can benefit by expanding their repertoire of media genres and design frames and building their portfolios. The presence of these students in StudioLab courses enhances the class experience for all, as they engage in peer-to-peer learning and teaching of particular design skills. Finally, although this book focuses on a specific set of tutor texts and takes inspiration from art-activist groups, potentially any subject matter or small productive team could be substituted. Transmedia knowledge, and StudioLab's three design frames in particular, can embrace any academic subject matter. If you doubt it, simply search the web for a specific field and different media forms (e.g., PechaKucha, comics, posters)—to see that specialized transmedia knowledge in that field already exists. StudioLab enables students to apply its design frames analytically and creatively in order to move from being a consumer to becoming a producer, collaborator, and world-maker of transmedia knowledge.

The curricular uses of StudioLab are many, and its critical design pedagogy can be incorporated into the curricular goals of any field or department. All fields want their students to communicate more effectively, which explains why colleges require first-year writing of all students and why departments often require additional, more specialized writing courses for graduation. StudioLab supplements these monomedia courses to give students transmedia knowledge-making and collaborative problem-solving skills—skills that complement rather than compete with writing and educational models based on coverage of information. Indeed, almost all the transmedia forms include writing and some other media. In short, they are themselves graphic multimedia: posters, websites, podcasts, theory comics—all of which involve alphabetic writing, which again is itself audiovisual.

But beyond communicating information, critical design and transmedia knowledge generate new ways of thinking and enable one to learn new ways of making arguments and new rhetorical strategies, while also opening up new evidence tracks. A traditional essay makes arguments and presents evidence solely through alphabetic writing. An illustrated essay or theory comic adds a visual track of evidence and introduces the possibility of nonlinear and narrative argumentation. A video essay or PechaKucha presentation can use both audio and visual evidence, and the layering of word, image, and sound, as well as simple or sophisticated transitions for argumentative and rhetorical effects.

In addition to enabling students to think differently and communicate their learning across media, StudioLab can also contribute to academic programs looking to adjust or revise their curriculum as a means to reach out to audiences and stakeholders beyond specialists. At a time when colleges and the liberal arts are publicly debating policymakers, the general public, and themselves about the value of their programs and requirements, administrators need both faculty and students to advocate and tell their stories regarding the value of higher education. Moreover, higher education needs to help society reimagine humans' place in the world. Efficacy, in particular, offers the liberal arts a different perspective on debates about the instrumentalization of knowledge, as it focuses on cultural and social ends, not just technical and economic. In response to attacks on the liberal arts and the humanities in particular, foundations and funding agencies such as NSF, Mellon, and the NEH, as well as alumni donors, have increased support for initiatives in public humanities, public history, public science, and community-and-service-based learning. Academic departments can develop StudioLab courses as part of their efforts for curricular innovation by transmediating their disciplinary knowledge into specific media forms to reach particular audiences. Obviously, revitalizing the liberal arts will not happen through one class, one pedagogy, one curricular innovation, or one institution. Nor will it happen overnight—structural, historical, and existential changes often unfold very slowly—until there is a crisis.

The Adventures of StudioLab

StudioLab Manifesto unfolds over the next three chapters to articulate three levels of transformational practice and engagement with the world, or what the French philosopher Gilles Deleuze calls different series of *becoming* or metamorphosis. These levels of transformation—becoming maker, becoming builder, becoming cosmographer—can be taught as levels of gaming: the adventures of each level building upon what comes before it, while also raising the stakes.

Chapter 2, Becoming Maker, transforms students from media consumers to makers of transmedia knowledge. The first step in democratizing digitality is making media beyond writing. Becoming maker builds on traditional modes of knowledge-making by moving away from practices that rely on field coverage, object analysis, and alphabetic writing only, and adding project-based production of transmedia knowledge for different audiences. Individual projects allow students to transmediate knowledge from their own fields, while collaborative projects allow them to integrate learning from different fields. To facilitate this first transformation, this chapter focuses on the shift from critical thinking to critical design and provides specific tools such as the CAT design frame and tutor texts through which to critique, reimagine, and produce knowledge differently.

Chapter 3, Becoming Builder, transforms individual makers of transmedia knowledge into builders of collaborative platforms and shared experiences. Students create as *critical design teams* based on the model of artist activist groups, garage bands, and start-ups, rather than the model of solitary Romantic genius. Using tactical media production as a central means of critical design, this chapter argues for the importance of creating media collaboratively in conceptual teams, aesthetic bands, and technical guilds whose activities map respectively into seminar, studio, and lab spaces. Building on the CAT design frame, Chap. 2 introduces the UX (user experience) design frame to help teams make shared experiences scalable and sustainable. The UX frame teaches students skills in experience design, information architecture, and information design. It is within critical design teams that experiential architectures emerge, capable of connecting with other collaborative platforms.

Chapter 4, Becoming Cosmographer, transforms collaborative builders into cosmographers or co-designers of worlds through community engagement, such as participatory research, citizen science, and public humanities. StudioLab's third level builds on the skills and frames of Chap. 3, to connect collaborative problem-solving to the wider audiences:

communities, policymakers, and other partners outside the academy. This chapter introduces the third design frame, design thinking or DT, whose iterative process of empathy, definition, ideation, prototyping, and testing, seek to attune human desirability, technical feasibility, and economic sustainability, or in StudioLab's performative terms, to valorize cultural efficacy in relation to technical effectiveness and organizational efficiency. Here we discover transmedia at the heart of all knowledge production.

StudioLab Manifesto issues three calls to adventure, repeated appeals to engage the battle for the liberal arts and reconfigure Plato's Fight Club through a series of missions: to democratize digitality, to democratize critical design, and to remix the performative values of efficacy, efficiency, and effectiveness. It also issues three calls to action: to become maker, to become builder, and to become cosmographer.

Learning StudioLab's design frames through sustained project work can be transformational, empowering one with creative confidence to bring critical design perspectives to other situations, including professional and life decisions. The CAT frame enables one to augment concept decision-making with cultural and technical nuances, and thus, dynamically redesign one's many different bodies of knowledge. The UX frame provides a language and practice to create such experiential transformations at intimate, interpersonal levels as well as larger social ones, while the DT frame provides a transdisciplinary, ready-made process for remixing values of efficiency and effectiveness with those of efficacy within communities and organizations.

Wrestling with Plato's Fight Club, StudioLab's critical design pedagogy produces not only conceptual arguments, aesthetic experiences, and technical processes found siloed across most campuses, it also mixes these activities to create cognitive-affective-material constellations of thought-action generated and shared through proposals, presentations, diagrams, prototypes, objects, apps, and other tactical media. At stake here is combining critical analysis and creative making at scale, and not just media making, but the building of transformative experiential architectures whose performance design extends from the internal dynamics of teams to those of collaborating groups and communities.

Emerging within seminar, studio, lab, and field spaces, from past, present, and future time zones, such experiential architectures give concrete form to the heterotopias envisioned by Foucault, as well as the columned academies of Plato. Such architectures provide intimate yet common platforms for the transvaluation of performative values and the actualization of possible worlds. Thus the adventure: *make media, build platforms, design worlds.*

REFERENCES

Bardzell, Jeffrey, and Shaowen Bardzell. 2013. What Is 'Critical' About Critical Design? In CHI '13 Proceedings of the SIGCHI Conference on Human Factors in Computing Systems, 3297–3306. New York: ACM.

Brown, Tim. 2009. Designers – Think Big! *TED: Ideas Worth Spreading*. Video. September. https://www.ideo.com/news/tim-brown-urges-designers-to-think-big-at-tedglobal

Derrida, Jacques. 1976. *Of Grammatology*. Trans. Gayatri Chakravorty Spivak. Baltimore: Johns Hopkins University Press.

Descartes, René. 1956. *Discourse on Method*. New York: Liberal Arts Press.

Docking, Jeffrey R. 2015. *Crisis in Higher Education: A Plan to Save Small Liberal Arts Colleges in America*. East Lansing: Michigan State University Press.

Dunne, Anthony, and Fiona Raby. 2016. *Critical Design FAQ*. http://www.dunneandraby.co.uk/content/bydandr/13/0. Accessed 1 Apr 2016.

Critical Art Ensemble. 2001. *Digital Resistance: Explorations in Tactical Media*. New York: Autonomedia.

Ferrall, Victor E. 2011. *Liberal Arts at the Brink*. Cambridge, MA: Harvard University Press.

Foucault, Michel, and Jay Miskowiec. 1986. Of Other Spaces. *Diacritics* 16 (1 Spring): 22–27.

Havelock, Eric Alfred. 1963. *Preface to Plato*. Cambridge, MA: Belknap Press/ Harvard University Press.

Lyotard, Jean-François. 1979. *The Postmodern Condition: A Report on Knowledge*. Trans. Geoffrey Bennington and Brian Massumi. Minneapolis: University of Minnesota Press.

Newfield, Christopher. 2008. *Unmaking the Public University: The Forty-Year Assault on the Middle Class*. Cambridge, MA: Harvard University Press.

Roth, Michael S. 2014. *Beyond the University: Why Liberal Education Matters*. New Haven: Yale University Press.

Spicer, André, Mats Alvesson, and Dan Kärreman. 2009. Critical Performativity: The Unfinished Business of Critical Management Studies. *Human Relations* 62: 537–560.

The Design Thinking Initiative. 2016. The Design Thinking Initiative. *Smith College*. Retrieved May 15, 2016. http://smith.edu/design-thinking/

Wickert, Christopher, and Stephan M. Schaefer. 2014. Towards a Progressive Understanding of Performativity in Critical Management Studies. *Human Relations*. 1–24. https://doi.org/10.1177/0018726713519279. First Published Online February.

Zakaria, Fareed. 2015. *In Defense of a Liberal Education*. New York: W.W. Norton & Company.

CHAPTER 2

Becoming Maker: Creating Transmedia Knowledge

Fig. 2.1 Still from "Cancer and Developing Countries." Kristel Joy Yee Mon. Video for vlog discussing graduate research in biomedical sciences. Cornell University (2017)

© The Author(s) 2019
J. McKenzie, *Transmedia Knowledge for Liberal Arts and Community Engagement*, Digital Education and Learning, https://doi.org/10.1007/978-3-030-20574-4_2

From Consumers to Makers

We consume media all the time: images, texts, and music flow through our smartphones and computers, but few of us become confident mediamakers. *Yet digital culture is a maker culture*, which means becoming both a critical consumer and a creative producer of different media forms. While we may capture and share photos and movies, our computers and handheld devices come loaded with software for editing and manipulating media that most people ignore, and the Internet offers an array of free website platforms that many do not even know about. Critical design is all about analyzing and creating media—from essays to videos to websites— and it begins with *becoming maker* (Fig. 2.1).

Traditionally, thinkers and makers have been sharply separated, with universities producing students who think and technical colleges producing students who do. Obviously, students at technical colleges think and those at liberal arts colleges and universities do, not only in Art, Physics, and Engineering but also English, History, and Sociology. But with the rise of maker culture, DIY movements, and digital culture more generally, the activities of designing and creating are blurring the boundaries between thinking and doing, as well as between different schools and disciplines. Innovation, invention, creativity—these activities are not restricted to entrepreneurs, inventors, and artists but are becoming democratized. Digital media accelerates this democratization process, and the role of critical design is to ensure that critical thinking remains a crucial dimension of democratizing digitality. To these ends, StudioLab extends critical thinking beyond writing to other media forms. Its critical design practices enable one to become a maker of transmedia knowledge.

But critical design is not just about making, it is about *why and for whom* we make—to express an idea? to move others? to change the world? Do we make only for specialists or also for community members, policymakers, and the general public? And critical design is also about *how* we make—effectively? efficiently? efficaciously? sullenly or joyfully? In one medium or many? In traditional genres and emerging ones? *Critical design asks: What are we making, how sustainable is it, and why and for whom are we making it in the first place?*

CRITICAL DESIGN 101: MAKING MEDIA

In order to democratize digital media, this chapter introduces the forms, activities, spaces, and one of the design frames at the heart of the StudioLab pedagogy. To help both faculty and students become makers within their fields, we start by exploring some tutor websites drawn from different disciplines. Tutor sites and other tutor materials offer heuristics, resources that can help one generate transmedia knowledge. We can learn from both their content and their form: don't steal or copy as much as emulate and create in their spirit.

Critical Design: Dunne and Raby

The first tutor site is that of designers Anthony Dunne and Fiona Raby, whose 2005 manifesto 'Towards a Critical Design' helps launch critical design as field by situating it precisely between *episteme* and *doxa*, expert discourse and popular media. This is the shared sweet spot of transmedia knowledge and critical design. Written to accompany Dunne and Raby's show *Consuming Monsters: Big, Perfect, Infectious* which dealt with issues surrounding biogenetics and designer babies, their manifesto argues that 'many issues are already being examined by ethicists and government organizations, the results usually take the form of highly technical, almost philosophical reports. When they are reported in the popular media it is often alarmist and sensational.'[1] At the same time, they contend that the potential of art, film, and literature to grapple with biogenetics and designer babies is undercut by their fictionalization and overdramatization of such issues. They counter: 'Products however, as a special category of object, can locate these issues within a context of everyday material culture. Design today is concerned with commercial and marketing activities, but it could operate on a more intellectual level, bringing philosophical issues into an everyday context in a novel yet accessible way.'[2]

---

[1] Anthony Dunne, and Fiona Raby, "Critical Design FAQ," retrieved April 1, 2016, http://www.dunneandraby.co.uk/content/bydandr/13/0.
[2] Idem.

36   J. MCKENZIE

Critical design, then, offers a speculative yet material mode of thinking that operates within the world itself. For Dunne and Raby, it is not just a matter of thinking critically about design but *thinking through the design and making of things and processes*. Critical design offers a mode of concrete speculative thought that is post-ideational and post-logical, in that it manifests itself in the world through hypothetical but nonetheless real objects and scenarios. 'Speculating through design by presenting abstract issues in the form of hypothetical products enables us to explore ethical and social issues within the context of everyday life.'[3] Likewise, for StudioLab, designing and making constitute a mode of thinking in its own right, a mode of thinking and acting in the world that works with materials and ideas to engage the full spectrum of mind, body, and spirit. It involves the making of what we will call *thought-action figures*. One creatively thinks-acts in StudioLab's critical design pedagogy, whether it be through the design of objects or events or processes. Critical design via transmedia knowledge requires thinking-acting across different media, engaging different senses and different cognitive skills. As we will see, speculative objects, counterfactual statements, and imagined worlds are part of StudioLab's pedagogy, and all can move toward becoming real world, high res, and highly concrete through iterative processes of transmediation. Doodles become buildings, diagrams become books.

The extension of critical thinking into critical design takes many paths, as colleges explore ways for students to combine writing and media through design. The development of design as a critical discourse in the US can be seen in academic courses and programs in *critical design thinking*, including a graduate degree at Virginia Tech University and an undergraduate initiative at Smith College, a liberal arts college in Massachusetts. As the name suggests, critical design thinking merges critical thinking and design thinking:

> The Smith brand of design thinking envisions design in service of broader social issues of participation, intervention and leadership. Design thinking can be used to question gender, power and ability as dynamics that shape who gets to participate in creating the world we live in.[4]

---

[3] Idem.

[4] The Design Thinking Initiative, Smith College, retrieved May 15, 2016, http://smith.edu/design-thinking/.

StudioLab's critical design mixes critical thinking, design thinking, and tactical media, and likewise seeks to prioritize values of cultural efficacy in relation to organizational efficiency and technical effectiveness. Critical design thinking, in particular, offers students concrete methods for site-specific micro-transvaluations of value, and it is important to note that Smith College's inaugural projects include a campus-wide initiative to rethink the college's work and learning spaces. From StudioLab's perspective, democratizing digitality requires changing values in order to transform the spaces, media, curricula, and organization of learning and empower students to approach knowledge and power in both critical and creative ways.

Digital Storytelling and StoryCenter

In recent years, digital storytelling has emerged as a powerful form for expressing experiences and ideas through video technologies. Our second tutor site is thus StoryCenter (originally the Center for Digital Storytelling), a leader in developing and bringing this form to individuals, communities, and organizations.

> We create spaces for transforming lives and communities, through the acts of listening to and sharing stories. Since 1993, we have partnered with organizations around the world on projects in StoryWork, digital storytelling, and other forms of digital media production. Our selection of public workshops supports individuals in creating and sharing stories.[5]

The basic process involves developing and recording a well-crafted story based on personal experience, storyboarding a simple yet compelling visual track of photos and/or videos, and then editing the audio and visual together into a short, powerful video. Through its workshops, StoryCenter has helped democratization digitality by teaching 20,000 people digital storytelling skills. In the US, storytelling in general has blossomed into a major social phenomenon, with both artists and institutions turning to it as a way to use intimate experiences to reveal large, social relations, or to enhance public relations. Alongside StoryCenter, Brandon Stanton's *Humans of New York* and the projects of the nonprofit StoryCorps use

---

[5] "About Storycenter," https://www.storycenter.org/about/, accessed March 23, 2018.

personal stories to reveal aspects of the human condition at the level of city and nation, respectively.

On another level, organizations and businesses have developed practices of transmedia storytelling (stories told across a variety of media: film, print, action figures, etc.) and strategic storytelling (stories told as part of strategic communication). Significantly, StoryCenter has recently partnered with the National Humanities Center to help create Humanities Moments, digital stories revealing the impact that humanities have had on individual lives—and thus the importance of humanities within contemporary culture. In our own mix of expert and common discourses, StudioLab embraces digital storytelling as a central way of introducing *mythos* and *imagos* (story and images), into discourses dominated by *logos* and *eidos* (logic and ideas), or to put this in another register, mixing common experience and formal knowledge to produce a new mode of thought and action. Stories are only one way to organize or 'architect' experiences and knowledge, and video only one digital form, but digital storytelling demonstrates how experience and knowledge can move across innumerable media, fields, and institutions.

Within traditional genres such as academic books and presentations, scholars regularly use stories and other narrative forms, often without realizing it. Sometimes, an anecdote will open a presentation, intended as a way to connect with the audience and introduce the topic. More substantively, any logical or rhetorical appeal to history or historical evidence, whether indirect or direct, appeals to a narrative unfolding of time which may range from a detailed account of a specific event to a sequence of related events to an overarching grand narrative—such as the Enlightenment or Progress. But it is not just historians and humanists who tell stories and make arguments about and with them: we also find narrative structures in case studies, lab reports, and descriptions of complex social phenomena and natural processes—Revolution, for instance, and Evolution. First this, then this, then this.

In *Houston, We Have a Narrative: Why Science Needs Story*, marine biologist Randy Olson argues that most scientists are terrible storytellers, and many resist even considering themselves as storytellers. However, he finds narrative at work in one of the most widely used textual structures in knowledge production, IMRAD, the structure of Introduction, Method, Results, and Discussion used in medical articles and other scientific publications. This structure was invented in the 1920s and widely adopted in the 1940s, but most scientists do not know the formal name IMRAD, nor

2 BECOMING MAKER: CREATING TRANSMEDIA KNOWLEDGE   39

recognize its three-part narrative structure, even though they use it routinely: beginning (I), middle (M&R), and end (D).[6] For Olson, scientists are simply poor storytellers, at a time when science needs story—and in our context, the liberal arts need digital storytelling.

For StudioLab, the most important insight here is that in addition to sharing personal experiences, stories can and do mix with arguments, and thus can also generate shared experiences of formal knowledge and conceptual understanding, even in the most traditional and rigorous of academic media, the scientific article. Moreover, stories can not only introduce arguments rhetorically and function as evidence, description, and overarching structure, *they also express the core activities of research and learning themselves:* discovery, method, interpretation, insight, realization, conceptualization, enlightenment, and so on. Descartes' *Discourse on Method,* after all, can be read as a *Bildungsroman* or coming-of-age story for both scientist and science itself. Kant makes this maturation the story of the Enlightenment. Significantly, Olson argues that the information explosion has led to a dramatic increase in publications *about* narrative, suggesting that storytelling offers a way to generate higher-level patterns of information.[7] From our perspective, the explosion of narrative research and the rise of science communication and strategic communication, as well as areas such as conceptual and data storytelling, all point to the emergence of digitality and its global mashup of orality and literacy, apparatuses of power and knowledge built on *mythos* and *logos,* story and logic. If we understand story and logic as two foundational modes of pattern-making that have guided human thought and action, the question arises: what new patterns emerge with the apparatus of digitality? Here critical design can help us think-act.

Improv Science and the Alda Center for Communicating Science

Our third tutor site directly addresses how scientists incorporate subjective, expressive, and even physical elements to communicate their specialized research with public audiences, policymakers, and the media. Focusing on the speaking body, the Alan Alda Center for Communicating

---

[6] Randy Olson, *Houston, We Have a Narrative: Why Science Needs Story* (Chicago: The University of Chicago Press, 2015), 6–8.

[7] Ibid.

Science at Stony Brook University teaches scientists and health professionals the basics of improvisation and other theatrical techniques. Named for actor Alan Alda, the 'Alda Center offers a range of instructional programs for science graduate students and scientists, including workshops, conferences, lectures, and coaching opportunities, as well as credit-bearing courses offered through the School of Journalism.'[8] Alda himself has helped develop the program whose 'goal of teaching scientists improv is not to turn them into actors, but to free them to talk about their work more spontaneously and directly, to pay dynamic attention to their listeners and to connect personally with their audience.'[9] Increasingly, scientists recognize the importance of nurturing and maintaining a positive relationship with both specialized and nonspecialized audiences, including policymakers and the general public, in part because their research largely depends upon grants from the National Science Foundation (NSF), the National Institutes for Health (NIH), and other funding sources. Indeed, NSF and NIH grant applications require researchers to describe the broader impact of their work, and while this component does not carry as much weight as the proposal's intellectual merit, the rise of community-based participatory research methods, on the one hand, and anti-science political forces, on the other, may cause both scientists and funding organizations to place more emphasis on the ways research affects local communities and society at large.

For StudioLab, the Alda Center demonstrates the power of bringing the performing arts studio-based practices to researchers working in a totally different environment, that of the science lab. Other hybrid forms of scientific knowledge include science rap and Dance Your PhD. As the name suggests, science rap translates scientific knowledge into rap music, with lyrics conveying specialized knowledge sung to hip-hop music. The form owes much to Tom McFadden, a science educator at the Nueva School in Hillsborough, California, who studied biology at Stanford and science communication at the University of Otago, New Zealand. Since 2011, McFadden's middle school students have created and published

---

[8] Alan Alda Center for Communicating Science, The Alda Center, accessed May 30, 2019, aldacenter.org.
[9] Ibid.

2 BECOMING MAKER: CREATING TRANSMEDIA KNOWLEDGE   41

music videos through the Science Rap Academy on YouTube,[10] and under the rubric of Science with Tom, he offers workshops teaching faculty to compose science rap in little under an hour.[11] Lest one thinks rap is only for school kids, A. D. Carson's 2017 doctoral dissertation at the University of Clemson took the form of a full-length rap album, *Owning My Masters: The Rhetorics of Rhymes & Revolutions*, which both studies and embodies the question of authentic black voices in academic sites—such as Clemson, a campus whose history is entwined with slavery. Revealing the troubling genealogies of 'mastery' that connect colonialism and formal education, Carson's performative dissertation is both site specific and virtual, grounded and mobile. Carson produced his critical race rap album for his degree in Clemson's innovative program in Rhetorics, Communication, and Information Design, and it is available online along with lyrics, texts, and videos.[12]

Like the performances of improv science and science rap, Dance Your PhD does precisely what it says, but on the sustainable scale of an annual international competition, sponsored by *Science Magazine* and the American Association for the Advancement of Science. Science journalist John Bohannon started the Dance Your PhD contest in 2008, and now each year doctoral students in four areas, Physics, Chemistry, Biology, and the Social Sciences, from around the world translate their research into dance.[13] Modern experimental dance, in particular, proves especially apt at transmediating advanced research into topics such as complex natural dynamics and biological processes, abstract mathematical structures, and human creativity and interaction by choreographing them into dance videos ranging from two to ten minutes.[14] This mixing of studio and lab

[10] Tom McFadden, "Science Rap Academy," *YouTube* video playlist, last updated July 26, 2018, accessed January 27, 2019, https://www.youtube.com/playlist?list=PLvgILFwoRX2min-PEDNXfk25KULkKfy7S&app=desktop.

[11] Tom McFadden, Science with Tom website, accessed January 27, 2019, https://www.sciencewithtom.com/.

[12] A. D. Carson, "Owning My Masters: The Rhetorics of Rhymes & Revolutions," accessed January 27, 2019, https://phd.aydeethegreat.com/.

[13] Wikipedia contributors, "Dance Your PhD," *Wikipedia, The Free Encyclopedia*, last modified December 3, 2018. https://en.wikipedia.org/wiki/Dance_Your_PhD.

[14] Jason Daley, "Watch the Winners of the 2017 Dance Your Ph.D. Competition," *Smithsonian.com*, November 3, 2017, accessed January 27, 2019. https://www.smithsonianmag.com/smart-news/watch-winners-2017-dance-your-phd-competition-180967068.

activities lies at the heart of StudioLab's pedagogy, informing not only the types of projects and media that students make but as we will see, the very space in which this making unfolds.

The hybrid genres of digital storytelling, improv science, science rap, and Dance Your PhD, all demonstrate that practices long excluded from knowledge production—theater, music, song, and dance—are reemerging inside the academy itself, far from their specialized fields and formal institutions. Poetry, music, song, and dance are practices Plato excluded from the Republic due to their enchanting mimetic effects on audiences, and their reemergence in science gives us insight into not only the hybrid forms that knowledge takes in digitality but also the transformations at stake in the thinking body itself.

Smart Media and DesignLab

A final tutor site here is DesignLab, a media design consultancy at the University of Wisconsin–Madison. DesignLab functions like a writing center for new media projects generated by student courses and research, as well as student organizations and other extra-curricular activities. It offers no classes of its own but provides one-on-one and group consultations, serving hundreds of students each term. A key contribution of DesignLab to critical design has been its formulation and description of *smart media* or emerging scholarly genres that supplement the traditional print genres of scholarly books and articles.[15] Smart media are transmedia knowledge and include multimedia presentation forms such as TED talks, PechaKucha, and PowerPoint presentations; video forms such as video essays and vlogs; digital images such as infographics, posters, and illustrations; and many other media genres already being used by scholars worldwide. Smart media are a primary form that critical design takes in StudioLab.

Yet resistance to such transmedia knowledge remains strong in Plato's Fight Club. A report of the 2010 Scholarly Communication Institute, *Emerging Genres in Scholarly Communication*, describes the alienating

---

[15] See Jon McKenzie, "Smart Media at the University of Wisconsin-Madison," (*Enculturation: A Journal of Rhetoric, Writing and Culture 15* http://www.enculturation. net/smart-media), and Jon McKenzie, "DesignLab & The Democratization of Digitally," TEDx University of Wisconsin, https://www.youtube.com/watch?v=YmYgTy2VkBU.

obstacles that come between humanities faculty and students when faced with digital media:

> The reliance of faculty on tenure and review models tied to endangered print genres leads to the disregard of innovation and new methodologies. And mobile, digitally fluent students entering undergraduate and graduate schools are at risk of alienation from the historic core of humanistic inquiry, constrained by outmoded regimes of creation and access.[16]

These same print genres constrain scientists and social scientists. Powerful disciplinary and infrastructural forces thus limit the democratization of digitality and the emergence of transmedia knowledge, forces closely tied to the logocentric origins of the modern university and its reluctance to imagine new institutional values. Beginning in the 1960s with mainframe computers and ARPANET (the Advanced Research Project Agency Network), the digital infrastructure has been installed in higher education for almost half a century, but while universities helped create today's Internet they struggle to compete with Apple, Google, and other corporations for students' time and attention. Transmedia knowledge comprises the means for addressing this lag between infrastructure (databases, networks, computers, and search engines) and superstructure (pedagogy, curriculum, research methods, tenure, and promotion standards) that helps structure the crisis of the liberal arts. Transmedia knowledge blurs Plato's distinctions of *logos* and *imagos*, *eidos* and *imagos*, *episteme* and *doxa*, and facilitates the emergence of a new, post-ideational mode of thinking and acting. *It is within a new makerspace of thought and action that new values must be forged, at the border of expert and common knowledge.*

DesignLab obviously did not invent the emerging scholarly genres but has carefully gathered them together and crafted 'smart media kits' that provide descriptions, examples, and tips and resources for creating them.[17] Within our StudioLab pedagogy, students regularly research a topic and over the course of a semester translate their knowledge into a suite of transmedia projects, for instance, a graphic essay, a multimedia presentation, a video essay, and a website that contextualizes and contains these

---

[16] Scholarly Communications Institute, http://uvasci.org/institutes-2003-2011/SCI-8-Emerging-Genres.pdf.

[17] University of Wisconsin-Madison, Smart Media, accessed July 7, 2016, designlab.wisc.edu/smart-media.

44   J. MCKENZIE

media forms. Similarly, workshop participants translate their own work into one or two transmedia genres. In both cases, the knowledge or content is actively shaped for different audiences. What's important to recognize here: StudioLab's transmedia knowledge for liberal arts entails neither a broadside critique of expert knowledge nor its noncritical dissemination to others, but rather, its strategic and tactical reinscription into transmedia knowledge attuned to different stakeholders—peers, community members, decision-makers, the general public—stakeholders essential to the accompanying transvaluation of values at the levels of institution and infrastructure. For this transvaluation to unfold, both students and faculty must become makers, and transmedia knowledge must become part—indeed the means—of campus and professional discussions about designing curricula and tenure standards that meet the challenges facing the liberal arts.

TRANSMEDIA KNOWLEDGE AND THE IMAGE OF THOUGHT

These tutor sites enable us to elaborate our definition of StudioLab's approach to critical design and to formalize the type of knowledge it produces. Students become makers by producing *transmedia knowledge*, knowledge that moves across different media in order to engage different audiences, rather than remaining limited to academic writing targeting only experts. Transmedia knowledge also mixes *episteme* and *doxa*, expert and common knowledge, by combining ideas and images, as well as logic and narrative, for a wide variety of effects: persuasive, communicative, educational, aesthetic, experimental, and so on. This knowledge is post-ideational as its thought extends beyond the production and analysis of ideas and logical arguments to also include the making of moods, images, stories, events, objects, environments. Emerging transmedia forms tend to be hybrid and multimedia—digital storytelling, science rap, info comics, Dance Your PhD, lecture performance—yet *all media become transmedia as thinking moves across media*. Thus, ideas and academic writing become transmedia knowledge in StudioLab—or rather their inherent transmediality comes to the fore: the alphabet, again, visualizes sound and enables the vocalization of script.

Alongside its new forms, the organization and dynamics of knowledge alter radically, at the root, with transmediation. The tree of knowledge, whose branching structure captures Aristotle's logical categories and the step-by-step movement of thought up and down as induction and deduction, becomes overgrown with the grasses and tubers described by Deleuze and Guattari, who contrast tree and rhizome as two images of thought.[18] The tree stands with its unity, verticality, and linear development; the rhizome spreads with its multiplicity, horizontality, and nonlinear breaks. Such rhizomatic organization and dynamics extend out into the world. Social scientists distinguish between hierarchical and networked organizations, making similar distinctions between their structure and movement of resources, information, and decision-making. In the natural world, geneticists have recently discovered that genetic materials not only flow vertically within a species from one generation to the next but also move transversally across different species through horizontal genetic transfer, a process that seems ubiquitous. What's important here is not to oppose these images of thought but to juxtapose and map their convergences and divergences, for trees become grasses and vice versa. Step-by-step thinking gives way to abductive leaps and conductive flashes, which open new spaces for other steps and leaps.

Transmedia knowledge entails new forms and arrangements of knowledge, and it also composes a new body for thought and action, a body produced in a variety of ways. Transmedia knowledge emerges through the combination of learning activities that involve different body movements and spatial configurations, those found in seminar, studio, lab, and field. Because transmedia knowledge foregrounds making, it consists of embodied know-how as well as intellectual know-what, bringing practice and theory into a new alignment. Critical thinking becomes critical design via transmediation. Moreover, as it multiplies media beyond text, to image, sound, objects, environments, and so on, transmedia knowledge engages many more senses and thus generates more sensations in its creation and reception than does ideational knowledge alone. And through the plasticity of new neural pathways, arborescent thought becomes rhizomatic. In these interconnected ways, thinking becomes post-ideational: if Rodin's sculpture *The Thinker* captures ideation in a seated, inwardly contemplative pose, in StudioLab the thinker becomes outwardly active and performs: she stands, plays music, sings, dances, makes media. Becoming maker, the thinker becomes thought-action figure.

---

[18] Gilles Deleuze and Felix Guattari, *A Thousand Plateaus* (Minneapolis: University of Minnesota Press, 1987), 1–25.

Thought-Action Figures and Media Cascades

With transmedia knowledge, a new image of thought emerges: thought-action figures, which are to digitality what ideas are to literacy, basic forms of thought and existence (recall that Plato interpreted Being as *eidos*). Thought-action figures are not limited to human figures: animals, plants, machines, systems, processes, materialities, symbols, and other abstract entities—all become thought-action figures via transmediation, movement through mediums deemed material, spiritual, cultural, and so on, within different ontologies, essentially different worlds. Design thinking researchers refer to 'media-cascades' as 'the sequence of representations through which projects develop and unfold in different media during the course of a development cycle,'[19] drawing on Bruno Latour's research on thinking with eyes and hands and the cascades of inscriptions, columns, files, and screens that comprise the production of knowledge.[20] Thought-action figures emerge not only in individual media but in their cascading movement across diverse media, their sometimes smooth, sometimes flickering, sometimes jagged transmediation of thought and action.

Moreover, in becoming maker, both thinking and thinker, action and actor enter into the cascade of transmediation, revealing the mind-body as a medium for rhythms, sounds, images, representations, technical routines, economic flows, moral systems, and so on. Thought-action figures operate both cognitively and affectively, working on the minds and bodies of makers as well as audiences: indeed, becoming maker entails reshaping one's thought and action, reinscribing the ideation and logic of Western thinking within a broader mediascape of stories and poetic structures, pictures and diagrams, melodies and refrains, rhythms and patterns, spaces and voids.

Media theorist D. N. Rodowick argues that new media and twentieth-century thinkers such as Lyotard, Deleuze, and Derrida have helped introduce the figural as a new historical mode of thinking that displaces the opposition of word and image within an emerging formation of power and knowledge.

---

[19] Jonathan Edelman and Rebecca Currano, "Re-representation: Affordances of Shared Models in Team-Based Design," in *Design Thinking: Understand – Improve – Apply, 61 Understanding Innovation*, ed. Hasso Plattner, Christoph Meinel, and Larry Leifer (Berlin & Heidelberg: Springer-Verlag, 2011), 61–79.

[20] Bruno Latour, "Visualisation and Cognition: Drawing Things Together," (*Knowledge and Society Studies in the Sociology of Culture Past and Present*, ed. H. Kuklick, Jai Press, 6, 1–40).

What is ultimately at stake is how the possibilities of knowledge are defined in relation to power in given historical epochs. These strata, or more precisely, their particular combination and distribution of visible and expressible, constitute the positive forms of knowledge as historical a prioris. There are only 'practices' of knowledge and strategies of power.[21]

For Rodowick, the figural emerges as a new arrangement of power-knowledge with societies of control (governed by performativity rather than disciplinarity) and digital media, and notably, he cites cyberpunk and guerrilla media as 'resisting, redesigning, and critiquing digital culture.'[22] For us, thought-action figures, like the ideas and writing of literacy, constitute *pharmakon*, undecidables whose effects of power and resistance turn around one another. Figures can be appropriated and expropriated—used and abused—by other forces as they cascade through different power setups. Exemplars of such figures from the sciences include Einstein's $e=mc^2$ equation, Watson and Crick's double helix DNA structure, and Mandelbrot's geometric fractals; from the human sciences, Nietzsche's eternal return, Wittgenstein's rabbit-duck, and Haraway's cyborg; from the history of activism, Gandhi's *khadi* clothing, ACT-UP's pink triangle, and the Guerrilla Girls' gorilla masks; and from corporate marketing, the Nike swoosh, McDonald's golden arches, and the Apple logo. Dance Your PhD and science rap are transmedia genres packed with thought-action figures. Overloaded with conceptual content and laden with emotional charge, such figures take shape in different contexts and their effects range from immediate 'shocks' to sharp or vaguely defined personae to silently evolving backgrounds and atmospheres.

In making thought-action figures and reinscribing ideas across media, StudioLab students approach transmedia knowledge not just tactically but also *tactilely*, actively handling and manipulating concepts, images, sounds, and other materials in order to explore their affordances and constraints, experimenting with the different functions that figures can support and the various effects they can produce across different media genres and contexts. What happens when an analytical paper is translated into a proposal for a local community installation, or when that proposal then takes the form of a multimedia presentation to a group of policymakers, or when the project subsequently becomes an actual installation and public event? The thought-action figures bend and stretch as they take different medial forms and affect different audiences in unforeseen ways.

---

[21] D. N. Rodowick, *Reading the Figural, or, Philosophy after New Media* (Durham, NC: Duke University Press, 2001), 54.

[22] Ibid., 234.

McLuhan famously wrote 'the medium is the massage' (in addition to it being the message), by which he meant that media work over the body's sensorium, just as a masseuse works over its muscles.[23] The 'working over' effected by transmedia knowledge thus extends throughout the traditional communication sequence of sender-message-receiver, rerendering it as a transversally haptic space of thought-action figuration. If we also note that dancer Yvonne Rainer once declared 'the mind is a muscle,'[24] we can say that transmedia knowledge exercises different cognitive and sensory muscles to elicit different thought-actions as students move through the learning activities of seminar, studio, and lab.

An essential element of StudioLab's critical design approach to democratizing digitality is obviously digital media itself: democratizing its making. Thought-action figures take shape through the making and sharing of transmedia knowledge. Everyday media forms such as public presentations, posters, and YouTube videos carry powerful communicative and affective force, while search engines, wikis, and other tools have transformed knowledge discovery and empowered communities to connect locally and globally. At their very best, even the most derided of media forms—for example, PowerPoint—can produce intelligent, sensitive effects for audiences intimate and massive: one thinks of Al Gore's 2006 *An Inconvenient Truth*, effectively an Academy Award–winning PowerPoint presentation, or Chai Jing's 2015 *Under the Dome*, a powerful documentary on pollution in China downloaded by hundreds of millions of viewers before being censored by the Chinese government. StudioLab's critical design approach uses transmedia knowledge to forge connections across spaces, disciplines, and communities. Yet while TED talks, digital storytelling, and similar media forms have become ubiquitous in the early twenty-first century, what is lacking has been a language for analyzing them and a practice for creating them in scalable, sustainable ways. Along with transmedia knowledge forms, our critical design frames play a crucial role here.

Design Frame 1: CAT

What does transmedia knowledge look, sound, and feel like? How can one describe it? And how does one make and evaluate the movement of thought-action across different media genres? StudioLab uses three design

---

[23] Marshall McLuhan and Quentin Fiore, *The Medium is the Massage* (New York: Bantam Books, 1967), 26.

[24] See Catherine Wood, *Yvonne Rainer: The Mind Is a Muscle* (London: Afterall, 2007).

frames to help students generate projects and enable both students and faculty to evaluate them. We introduce the first design frame here, Conceptual/Aesthetic/Technical, which we abbreviate as CAT. CAT combines three aspects or dimensions of transmedia knowledge production:

- *Conceptual*: the guiding argumentative, expressive, rhetorical, or experimental content of the media
- *Aesthetic*: the visual, aural, textual, and interactive qualities of media embodying this content
- *Technical*: the selection, combination, and use of tools and techniques to produce the media

The CAT frame can be used to describe, analyze, and generate transmedia knowledge or any media work for that matter. CAT enables us to describe both individual media genres and, more importantly, the ways in which movement across media forms affects conceptual, aesthetic, and technical dimensions. As most writers, engineers, designers, and artists know, in practice the distinctions between conceptual, aesthetic, and technical dimensions can be difficult to unravel, especially when working in a single medium. However, with transmediation, these dimensions emerge and become malleable. Often, the conceptual content remains stable, the aesthetic affect can shift dramatically depending on audience, and the technical means change significantly.

We can describe the traditional academic essay using the CAT frame. The essay's C is its argument and evidence, its *logos*, and its rhetorical appeal to *ethos* and *pathos*. Disciplinary training and research supply the conceptual content, with arguments and evidence found and produced with recognized methods and protocols. The academic essay's A is its writing style, which typically strives for clarity and cohesion, qualities attained by a contextualizing introduction, an orderly sense of transition and building between paragraphs and sections, and a conclusion that gathers the main arguments and closes with implications and/or further questions. Aesthetics here also includes something so ingrained that we barely notice it: the text's layout and physical support, that is, 8.5 × 11-inch white paper, black 12-point font, and 1-inch margins. The essay's T is often Microsoft Word or similar word-processing software—whose default settings produce this layout—plus the computer hardware, and any other technologies used in the essay's composition: books, search engines, pencil and paper, camera, and so on. First-year writing courses effectively

50   J. MCKENZIE

teach students this CAT framework for critical thinking, instructing them to present arguments and evidence in clear prose. Significantly, most colleges assume students already know how to use computers, know Microsoft Word, and provide access to computer labs, if needed.

Redesigning Silence

StudioLab challenges students to transmediate knowledge by learning new aesthetic and technical skills and developing new muscles for conceptual development, as different transmedia genres entail different configurations of CAT. To see and hear CAT in thought-action across media, we can explore another set of tutor materials: a suite of transmedia knowledge produced by Steel Wagstaff, a graduate English student at the University of Wisconsin–Madison. In a course on Future Learning, students were asked to transmediate a research paper that they had written in one of their other courses (again, StudioLab can engage potentially any subject matter). While other students chose papers on such topics as animal rights, science communication, and feminist film, Wagstaff selected a research paper on American composer and writer John Cage titled *Essays into Silence, Noise, and John Cage*.[25] The C or conceptual content of the paper consists of the argument and textual evidence. In terms of aesthetics, Wagstaff had produced a traditionally formatted seminar paper divided into three topical sections although he had already generated a variation inspired by Cage: he called the sections 'movements' and introduced noise into the body of the text by gradually writing longer and longer footnotes. In short, Wagstaff had used Cage's work as tutor material, subtly experimenting with the academic essay's form. Technically, he produced the text using a common word-processing program.

Assigned a StudioLab project to transmediate his seminar paper into a *graphic essay*, Wagstaff learned Photoshop and InDesign in our lab workshops and then spent studio time reconfiguring his seminar paper by breaking up the text into different page layouts, exploring different fonts, sizes, and color, and most importantly, adding a visual track of photographs, diagrams, and other images, both as figures and in the background. The result was a graphic essay, also divided into three movements, produced in the style of a zine or a homemade, small circulation magazine (Fig. 2.2).

---

[25] Steel Wagstaff, unpublished paper. He describes the project in "The {Silence} Project: Some Adventures in Remediation," *Enculturation* 15. Published: September 27, 2012. Accessed July 9, 2018. http://www.enculturation.net/essays-into-silence-noise-and-john-cage.

2 BECOMING MAKER: CREATING TRANSMEDIA KNOWLEDGE   51

Fig. 2.2 Selections from seminar paper, graphic essay, and video, "The{Silence} Project: Some Adventures in Remediation." (Steel Wagstaff 2012)

The Conceptual-Aesthetic-Technical configuration of Wagstaff's graphic essay differs dramatically from that of his seminar paper. While the conceptual content remains largely unchanged, it has been reshaped and expanded by the aesthetic potential of the zine and the technical affordances of Photoshop and InDesign. Previously footnoted stories and facts enter into the main body of the zine, appearing in a diverse array of fonts and colors. The visual images open up an entirely new evidence track composed of photographs, diagrams, and graphic design elements, while the magazine layout and use of typography enable a fragmented and nonlinear reading experience inspired by Cage's use of chance, elements of everyday life, and other Fluxus art techniques. Using Cage's work as tutor material and emulating the Fluxus breakdown of the art/life divide, Wagstaff also mixed images of Cage with elements of contemporary visual culture and his own life. Photoshop and InDesign enabled him to use montage and the overlaying of image and text, basic aesthetic techniques of modernist art and design that contribute to the conceptual remake of his seminar paper. Anticipating our discussion of the second UX design frame in the next chapter, the different CATs have different targets and intended effects: while the seminar paper targets a highly specialized audience and produces a detached reading experience, the graphic essay genre of the zine entails a very different audience and reader experience: readers of noncommercial magazines passionately, even fanatically, devoted to counter-cultural topics ('zine' derives from fanzines).

A second transmediation of Wagstaff's essay, this time into a video essay, entails yet another CAT configuration and another set of users and affects. The conceptual component again follows the seminar paper closely, with the video divided into three topical movements. Aesthetically, the video essay's image track draws heavily on images from the graphic essay, while adding many other found images. Movement now enters literally through moving images: Wagstaff used pans, zooms, and animation features found in another technical tool, that of Apple's iMovie software. But the most noticeable and powerful conceptual, aesthetic, and technical difference between the video and both the paper and zine lies in the addition of yet another evidence track; the audio track, thus directly introducing into the CAT configuration the primary experiences whose distinctions Cage experimented with throughout his art/life: those of music, sound, noise, and silence. Not only do we hear Cage's voice, we hear an actual recording of *4'33"*, his most famous and controversial composition, performed and recorded by the BBC Symphony Orchestra. The silence, the noise, the music, is the sound of the audience breathing, coughing, and squirming in their seats. In addition, Steel creates an entire soundtrack composed of contemporary music, voices, and found sounds. He uses the technical affordances of the video-editing software to overlay image, sound, and text to make his conceptual argument 'more sound' by emulating and transforming the aesthetic (or anti-aesthetic) dimension of Cage's Fluxus life/work. The video genre opens up a wider set of audiences and experiences, as Wagstaff's video could be shown in public museums and on television, or posted online. Through this small suite of transmedia genres, we see the power of maker culture in transmedia knowledge production and the flexibility of the CAT design frame. Again, critical design and media do not replace critical thinking and writing: *they translate and mix them with other media forms in order to make them more effective and accessible to different audiences.* Transmedia knowledge enables new types of argumentation not limited to induction and deduction, but also including abduction (conceptual leaps within a domain) and conduction (pattern recognition across domains). It also provides a wider and richer combination of evidence tracks: not only textual, but also visual, audio, and interactive. At the same time, alongside expert knowledge, transmedia knowledge introduces *doxa* or common knowledge: images, sounds, and stories from popular culture, counterculture, and personal experience. This mix of expert and common knowledge within different media genres enables transmedia knowledge to engage a wide range of audiences, from experts to nonspecialists, from peers to community members to policymakers. Such transmedia knowledge production can generate a wide array of experiences and rhetorical effects: from detached and serious to dramatic and moving to humorous and light, depending on the target audience, intended effect, and CAT configuration.

Teaching Critical Design Frames

How to teach and learn StudioLab's critical design frames? StudioLab is project-based pedagogy: students learn the CAT, UX, and Design Thinking frames by designing and making transmedia knowledge to engage different audiences in different ways. The thought-action figures of projects appear differently through the three design frames, and students can learn CAT, UX, and DT separately or in different sequences. We often start with the CAT frame and do so here because its formal and functional simplicity opens up the making process to those who crave creative confidence but lack creative experience. CAT enables one to start making quickly and rigorously. The frame's simplicity is deceptive, as it accesses and connects conceptual, aesthetic, and technical dimensions of mind-boggling complexity while simultaneously enabling students to begin navigating them in exciting ways that they can share and discuss.

From a faculty's perspective, CAT's complex simplicity also makes it extremely versatile in the classroom. Here are some ways to begin teaching with the first design frame, ways that can also be used with UX and DT.

1. *Assign a transmedia project* that involves creating at least two media forms, such as a paper and a video or a presentation and a website, forms that connects specific content with specific audiences. While this could mean adding a new media form, many if not all disciplines already regularly assign transmedia projects, such as class presentations and poster projects, aimed at disciplinary audiences, even if little or no instruction in their aesthetic and technical dimensions occurs. Thus, one can add new media genres or build on existing assignments by formalizing and diversifying their target audiences, production, and evaluation. Explicitly state that you will evaluate the project using the CAT design frame, even if you don't formally teach it.

2. *Use CAT to plan class activities:* even without teaching the frame formally, plan to spend time *discussing* the conceptual components of the project; then spend time *looking, listening, and/or interacting* with examples, using them as tutor materials to learn their aesthetic dimension, how the content is shaped for the given media; also set aside for technical *skill-building*, whether it be software training or instruction in presentation or creating installations. Then provide time across several classes for students to actively integrate the conceptual, aesthetic, and technical components.

3. *Teach the frame both abstractly and concretely* by defining its three components, then demonstrating it by analyzing the conceptual, aesthetic, and technical aspects of different works with the same content—such as novels and film adaptations, or science textbooks and museums—and then asking students to do CAT analyses of works they select on their own. Like any analytic frame, students learn best by applying CAT repeatedly.

4. *Then ask students to plan their projects* by explicitly outlining the CAT configurations of their deliverables, just as they would plan and

outline a paper, an experiment, or a research project. This shift from analysis to synthesis defines critical media design: critical analysis in necessary but insufficient: critico-creative making is essential. Given the different transmedia genres, these plans could take the form of outlines, storyboards, flowcharts, prototypes, and production schedules. Have them review their plans in groups and with you.

5. *Ask students to make* transmedia using these CAT plans as blueprints for transmediating knowledge across media forms. Have this media production be both homework and classwork. As noted above, set aside several classes for making, and have students discuss their work in progress and provide feedback to them using CAT. Also discuss their progress vis-à-vis their plans, adjusting the latter if necessary.

6. *Ask students to present their transmedia knowledge* before the class and require students to role-play as a target audience and discuss or 'crit' the work using the CAT frame: What is happening conceptually? Is the aesthetic dimension appropriate to the target audience(s)? What is the work's technical strengths and weaknesses?

7. *Explicitly evaluate the transmedia knowledge projects using the CAT frame*: use CAT as a rubric to read across the different forms, evaluating the conceptual, aesthetic, and technical strengths and weaknesses of each work. Alternatively, focus on each work separately and break down its CAT.

In practice, the simplicity of CAT quickly opens up to the complexity of its components. The conceptual dimension is constituted by the diversity and complexity of disciplinary knowledge itself, with its hundreds of specialized fields of objects, their established and emerging methodologies and infrastructures, and their various schools and genealogies. Typically, formal, conceptual knowledge is primarily the concern of researchers, instructors, and advanced students. The aesthetic dimension can be just as specialized and conceptual, whether components come from film, graphic design, painting, or other fields of visual culture; from musicology, sound design, and sound studies; from poetry and narrative; from theatre and performance art; from game design and virtual worlds. And technical languages include the burgeoning number of software, programming languages, social media platforms, and SDKs, as well as the technical dimension of computers, handheld devices, servers, and networks.

Such complexity may appear as a major challenge to the democratization of digitality. Yet this challenge is precisely that facing the liberal arts and higher education in the contemporary world. Specialized knowledge has always floated in a sea of common knowledge, and engagements between *episteme* and *doxa* are many. Community-based research, teaching, and service have sought to connect epistemic knowledge with local communities. Similarly, scholars and administrators have a long history of interacting with policymakers, public funding agencies, and private foundations; while popular science, public history, and public humanities have engaged the general public. In terms of aesthetics, information designer David McCandless suggests that exposure to popular culture gives us all 'a kind of dormant design literacy.' We exercise aesthetic judgment and creativity every day when we express ourselves verbally, when we make choices about food, gifts, and entertainment. Each morning we dress ourselves and go out without appearing as clowns in public. We likewise interact with interfaces and navigate digital spaces using devices that range from consumer to prosumer to professional grade. What we lack are common frameworks for bridging our technical skills, dormant design aesthetics, and formal conceptual languages. CAT provides a bridge for doing so, and at one level, StudioLab seeks to create educational contexts and opportunities for students to connect their academic learning, their everyday sense of style, and the media tools whose icons sit largely untouched on their laptops and iPhones. That's how simple becoming maker can be taught: assign transmedia projects, help students design them, and support their making.

Sleepy CATs in Disciplinary Homes: Why, What, and How

Responding to the crisis of the liberal arts entails redesigning the experience of specialized knowledge for diverse audiences. The CAT design frame helps to enable this redesign: indeed, CAT itself constitutes an animated thought-action figure. We can understand this animation by starting with specialized training. Given its transdisciplinary and cross-campus components, the dimensions of conceptual, aesthetic, and technical appeal and appear differently to faculty and students according to their respective training in seminars, studios, and labs. *Yet all scholars have their own CATs which rule their disciplinary homes*—that is, disciplinary training involves a set of conceptual systems and methods, an aesthetic of clarity and coherence, and technical tools and techniques for research, writing, and presentation. One might ask whether we teach our CATs or our CATs teach us. In terms of media design, these CATs perform well enough when writing peer-reviewed articles or class papers or, similarly, delivering conference or class presentations. However, 'well enough' varies from brilliant to engaging to so-so to boring across all fields, and many faculties readily admit that reading student papers and listening to peers' conference presentations can sometimes be, well, uninspiring experiences. And the effect on nonspecialists can be much more telling, ranging from incomprehension, frustration, and anger to disbelief and even pity. A thought-action figure emerges: that of the isolated ivory tower.

A specialized knowledge's dominant CAT configurations, its longstanding fix of conceptual, aesthetic, and technical components, can easily be stirred without bringing down the academy, yet for disciplinary reasons we prefer to let sleepy CATs lie rather than wake them and ourselves up to other shared experiences of knowledge. To stir sleepy CATs, StudioLab focuses much of its attention on the frame's aesthetic dimension. As we saw with Wagstaff's *Essays into Silence, Noise, and John Cage*, the conceptual dimension of transmedia knowledge often remains stable in transmediation, and while the technical tools shift, the most profound transformations can occur in the aesthetic dimension. In this context, *aesthetics entails massaging, shaping, and sometimes generating material (whether it be textual, visual, aural, or interactive) appropriate to the technical affordances of a given transmedia genre, as well as the expectations and experience base of target audiences.* When transmediating a paper into conference presentation, images are key; when making a podcast for a general audience, environmental audio can create an immersive atmosphere; when creating an installation for a community group, images, objects, and interactive elements can produce a multisensory environment. And at each stage, the look and feel, the rhythms, colors, and overall style may change. Such aesthetic choices enable ideas to morph through the medium's technical affordances and create a richer conceptual experience for the audience, whether specialized or nonspecialized. This morphing animates ideas into thought-action figures capable of moving audiences' minds and bodies.

Yet it is not a matter of simply adding new aesthetic and technical components, for the resulting transmedia knowledge also needs a shape, rhythm, or movement—that is, a well-crafted thought-action figure—that resonates with oneself and others, especially nonspecialists whose expectations and senses have not been trained by specialized CATs. Engaging with other audiences, the conceptual component may be recast to reveal contexts, connections, and even uses overlooked or unforeseen by the maker. Passing through academic paper, zine, and audio-video, silence itself becomes a thought-action figure, something composable and decomposable—which is precisely Cage's revelation and art/life method. Such discovery lies at the heart of human-centered design; for resonance works two ways, and the aesthetic and technical components can help audiences and makers tune each other in through the conceptual components. Thus, it is not a question of dumbing down conceptual knowledge but of building shared experiences that bridge *episteme* and *doxa*, expert and common knowledge. Makers and users learn from one another, and there are innumerable ways to do this.

We can visualize one way to craft resonant thought-action figures by turning to Lee LeFever's *The Art of Explanation*,[26] which uses a spectrum to diagram the distance separating Geeks and non-Geeks, in our terms, those with specialized, epistemic knowledge and those with common knowledge or *doxa* (Fig. 2.3). We find such distances between Town and Gown, city streets and conference rooms, policymakers and experts. LeFever argues that overcoming this distance depends on recognizing the difference between Why and How. Highly specialized discussions, such as those in colleges and academic conferences, tend to focus primarily on the How of argumentation, methodology, and specialized discourse, whereas the art of explanation requires also providing the Why, the discussion's broader significance, context, and stakes. For specialists, the Why is largely assumed and thus implicit—or even beyond question: 'of course, biology matters,' 'of course, we must study Shakespeare,' 'of course, history is

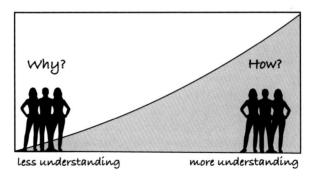

Fig. 2.3 Diagram based on the *Art of Explanation* by Lee LeFever (2012)

[26] Lee LeFever, *The Art of Explanation* (Hoboken, NJ: Wiley, 2012).

important!' The very existence of colleges and conferences embodies the legitimating context, and for many specialists, only children or philistines would ask Why? 'Can't they understand that the stakes are knowledge, culture, even civilization itself?' But for nonspecialists, the context and stakes are not self-evident and must be explained: the Why is lacking. Moreover, different specialists and even subspecialists in adjacent fields require the Why.

The solution offered by LeFever to bridge the gap between more and less understanding: Geeks must move along the spectrum toward non-Geeks and begin with the Why. Make the context and stakes clear from the start. LeFever then suggests telling a story (*mythos*) that guides attention from the contextual establishing shot toward the 'What' or main argument (*logos*). One then connects the story to the conceptual argument by interpreting the story as an illustration, case, or allegory of the What. Only after contextualizing, narrativizing, and connecting the Why to the What does one begin describing the How. For instance, in Plato's *Phaedrus*, Socrates begins by taking the young sophist outside the city walls of Athens. There, he tells Phaedrus the myth of Egyptian King Cadmus, who rejected the god Thoth's invention of writing for being detrimental to memory and thought. Connecting the myth to his argument, Socrates interprets the story as showing the superiority of *logos* over *graphe*, before describing the technique—the How—of dialectical reasoning.

Focusing on the Why of specialized knowledge can help recast the conceptual component, attuning it to both maker and audience. But transmedia knowledge, like traditional knowledge, does more than just explain. Beyond explanation, LeFever's Why-What-How distinctions can inform other processes, such as advocacy, decision-making, design, and problem-solving. Moreover, we can use it with respect to different audiences, as different stakeholders bring different contexts and perspectives—different Whys. And if we expand How to include not just internal details and processes but also the different ways various stakeholders can augment the What (e.g., how they can contribute to collaboration, implementation, publicity, funding, policy), we realize there may be different Hows as well as different Whys. In short, transmedia knowledge can help reveal different contexts and applications, different values and potentialities, all of which can help makers approach the What—the conceptual component of their transmedia knowledge—in more open and refined ways. This revelatory opening and refinement is the very opposite of 'dumbing down' specialized knowledge, and again it forms the heart of human-centered design, the place where *episteme* and *doxa* shape one another.

60   J. MCKENZIE

The Why-What-How structure can help faculty and students stir up sleepy ivy-towered CATs in order to craft thought-action figures that resonate with different audiences and stakeholders. In terms of transmedia knowledge production, Why-What-How can inform the composition of arguments in papers and presentations, narratives in digital stories and info comics, the visual layout of posters and installations, and even three lines of an elevator pitch. Thought-action figures, though captured by individual media forms, emerge precisely by passing through different iterations, jumping, shifting, and becoming animated in different ways as they appear within different media and contexts. This nonlinear transmediation is what make figures dynamic multiplicities rather than static units of ideation (though ideas are themselves never fixed in writing or thought—thus the history of philosophical thinking). Though only one way to choreograph experiences of transmedia knowledge, the steps of Why-What-How can help guide and shape the movement of thought-action figures both within and across different media forms.

Sparklines and the State of Bliss

Becoming maker via transmedia knowledge production has no one true method but follows or pathbreaks its way by any means necessary. Methods bring objects step by step before subjects as clear and distinct ideas. But as Heidegger contends in *The Age of the World Picture*, modern scientific explanation proceeds by mapping the unknown into the known. StudioLab's critical design process, however, involves using CAT and transmedia knowledge to remix *episteme* and *doxa* in order to open up the unknown within the known, so as to question it, critique it, defamiliarize it, recontextualize it, and/or create with it. When immersed in transmedia knowledge, ideation becomes a medium for generating thought-action figures capable of moving and transforming both Geeks and non-Geeks.

As we have seen, the remix of *episteme* and *doxa* (expert and common knowledge), *logos* and *mythos* (logic and story), and *eidos* and *imagos* (idea and image) lies at the heart of transmedia knowledge and critical design. It also beats in the heart of CATs between conceptual, aesthetic, and technical dimensions. Bertolt Brecht's Epic Theater similarly sought to both instruct and entertain, while Antonin Artaud's Theater of Cruelty combined metaphysics and an affective athleticism. Significantly, in her book *Resonate: Creating Visual Stories That Transform Audiences*, Nancy Duarte

Article	Presentation	Story
Written explanation of ideas and evidence	Oral delivery to explain and persuade	Artistic presentation of emotion and experience
Logical, argumentative	Facts and storytelling	Dramatic/narrative plot
Interpret, analyze, evaluate	Illuminate, interpret	Experience, express, sense
Findings, evidence	Motivation, engagement	Memories, associations
Clear, simple style	Believable, engaging	Expressive, theatrical

Fig. 2.4 Table based on *Resonate* by Nancy Duarte (2010)

defines multimedia presentations as combining elements of factual reports and artistic stories.[27] Her table can be revised to compare scholarly articles and gain insights into the recombinant nature of transmedia knowledge (Fig. 2.4).

A professional communication consultant, Duarte advised Al Gore on his film *An Inconvenient Truth*. In her work, she incorporates narrative theory and visual communication. Reworking Edmund Tufte's concept of graphical 'sparkline,'[28] Duarte has developed an influential presentation form featuring a narrative sparkline, a structure she finds at work in live presentations ranging from Martin Luther King, Jr.'s 'I Have a Dream' speech to Steve Jobs' original iPhone pitch (Fig. 2.5). In simplified form, Duarte's narrative sparkline has two dimensions. Horizontally, it moves left to right from beginning to middle to end, following the classic three-act structure found in dramas, novels, and popular films: set up/confrontation/resolution. Vertically, she defines two levels which the sparkline alternates between: a base 'what is' (the current situation) and a higher 'what could be' level (an imagined future). Over the course of the presentation, the presenter's goal is not to explain, instruct, or lecture but rather transport audiences from 'what is' or the set up to 'what could be,' the resolution that Duarte characterizes as a 'state of bliss.' The sparkline's

---

[27] Nancy Duarte, *Resonate* (Hoboken, NJ: Wiley, 2010).

[28] Tufte defines sparklines as 'data-intense, design-simple, word-sized graphics.' See *Beautiful Evidence* (Cheshire CT: Graphics Press, 2006), 47–63.

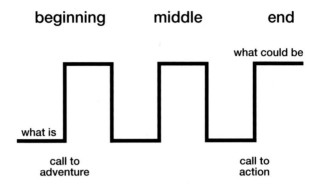

Fig. 2.5 Diagram based on *Resonate* by Nancy Duarte (2010)

beginning section ends with 'turning point 1,' an explicit 'call to adventure' that asks audiences to embrace the challenge of moving from 'what is' to 'what could be,' while the closing section begins with 'turning point 2,' a 'call to action,' an explicit appeal for the audience to take specific action to reach the state of bliss.

In the sparkline's longer middle section, Duarte situates a series of contrasts between What Is and What Could Be: this confrontation between present situation and possible future resonates with the audience's desire for transformation, whether it be personal or organizational. She also recommends inserting STAR moments (Something They'll Always Remember), such as a startling piece of evidence, a memorable anecdote, or a funny acronym, so the audiences can take away an experience that leads them back into the entire presentation. (The ancient arts of memory likewise employ striking images that aid the construction and delivery of arguments.) Duarte's sparkline is thus a resonance machine whose rhythms allow presenters to tune into audience expectations and experience base, their plans and desires—and then spark a transformation. The calls to adventure and action derive from the Hero's Cycle, a mythic archetype developed by Joseph Campbell and then extensively used by Hollywood scriptwriters for blockbusters from *Star Wars* to *Frozen*. These calls are directed to the hero of the story: in the case of presentations and other transmedia genres, *the protagonist is the audience*. Duarte stresses that *the audience is the hero of the story we share with them.*

Situating the audience as the hero resonates strongly with the desire of liberal arts colleges to communicate their value to diverse audiences, especially communities and policymakers. Reversing and displacing the opposition between *episteme* and *doxa*, the expert Geek is not the protagonist, the non-Geek is. We Geeks become sidekicks, helpers, co-creators in others' quests. This transformation of the specialist's role has profound implications for specific community-based research projects and, more generally, for the function of higher education in contemporary society. In the modern grand narratives described by Lyotard, scholars pose as heroes (or sometimes anti-heroes) of society; engaging postmodern optimization matrices, critical designers work alongside others critiquing power setups, identifying paradoxes and injustices, and inventing new collaborative ways to inject values of cultural efficacy into social systems obsessed with organization efficiency and technical effectiveness.

How to concretize the efficacy of foregrounding the Why within a narrative sparklines? In StudioLab workshops, participants sometimes bring their laptops, a current project, and a set of images. After learning the CAT design frame, LeFever's spectrum, and Duarte's sparkline, they transmediate their project into a PowerPoint, poster, or PechaKucha using LeFever's spectrum and Duarte's sparkline, whose reconfigured diagrams we overlay for them (Fig. 2.6):

The simple overlay demonstrates McLuhan's insight that in an age of information overload, all we have left is pattern recognition, the spark of conductive logic. Let's look at some patterns in our recombinant diagram. Starting on the lower left, the side of less understanding, we see that LeFever's *context* coincides with Duarte's introductory What Is, and that

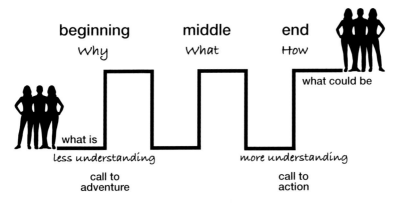

Fig. 2.6 Diagram based on Duarte (2010) and LeFever (2012)

Duarte's *call to adventure* and *first turning point* entail a *story* that conveys LeFever's Why and also introduces the audience to the *gap* separating them from What Could Be. The story delivers the stakes and significance of the presentation and serves as the entryway into the presentation's main body. In the middle sections, the contrasts between What Is and What Could Be work to introduce the main argument (the What), first through *connections* to the story, and then through direct *descriptions.* Finally, Duarte's second turning point, the call to action, occurs fully in the How. This How functions in two ways: it explains the details of the What and presents concrete steps the audience can take to overcome the gap and reach What Could Be.

In StudioLab workshops, participants commonly take 30 minutes to articulate and sketch the Why-What-How of their work into a narrative sparkline for multiple audiences. As they wrestle with their ideas, stretching their own mental muscles, they are becoming makers, thinkers making themselves thought-action figures.

WHAT COULD BE: A DANCING PLATO

Imagine this sparkline: The What Is is Plato's Fight Club amidst the crisis of liberal arts, higher education fighting for its place in the contemporary world, while What Could Be is a new configuration of *episteme* and *doxa,* campus and community, education and life. *StudioLab Manifesto* issues a call to adventure, initially captured broadly in the figure of Plato wrestling first with poetry and sophistry and later, through his Academy's legacy, with indigenous knowledges, popular cultures, and now digitality as the reinscription of oral and literate apparatuses within sociotechnical networks of material and digital flows. The call to action: use StudioLab to transform the critical thinking and writing of specialists into the critical design and transmedia knowledge of multiple players: specialists, local community members, policymakers, and the general public.

Moving across this imagined sparkline, we articulate StudioLab's call to adventure chapter by chapter through its three missions, having just begun with the first one: to democratize digitality, to build on the liberal arts' long-standing contribution to democratizing literacy within the context of a new apparatus of power and knowledge. Here, the call to action is 'become maker,' enable the self-transformation of passive media consumers into active producers of transmedia knowledge. In relation to ideational knowledge, transmedia knowledge entails a new image of thought and a new figure of the thinker. The thinker stands up, tries out some steps, makes some media. Animating the ideas of literacy, becoming maker produces dynamic thought-action figures. Becoming maker is becoming thought-action figure, remaking thought-action oneself. What could be? For starters, let us imagine a dancing Plato, freed from the opposition between earthly and cosmic music. This opposition assigned the muses of music-making and dance to *Gymnasium* while elevating *mouiske* in higher education to the Harmony of the Spheres, to forms, number, ratio—in short, to a *musica speculativa* that harmonizes *eidos* and *logos* on micro- and macrocosmic scales. Overcoming the dangerous excesses of local music and dance traditions with Pythagorean geometry, this cosmic choreography constituted the heights of Plato's Academy.[29]

Yet now, in a basement symposium near the city walls, Plato is partying with wrestlers, rhapsodists, and outcasts. He turns up the bass and switches on a Cagean noise machine with Mandelbrot projector. The patterns defy logic. They've discovered the secret to theory is a good set of subwoofers. As rhythm overcomes melody, Plato's symposium transmediates *The Republic* into a video for the Dance Your Discipline competition.[30] Beyond making, what sorts of collaboration does such a scene entail? What sort of world could this be? Those of builders and cosmographers.

References

Alan Alda Center for Communicating Science, The Alda Center, accessed May 30, 2019, aldacenter.org.

Carson, A.D. 2017. *Owning My Masters: The Rhetorics of Rhymes & Revolutions*. A Dissertation for the Graduate School at Clemson University. https://phd.aydeethegreat.com/. Accessed 12 Apr 2018.

Daley, Jason. 2017. Watch the Winners of the 2017 Dance Your Ph.D. Competition, Smithsonian.com, November 3. https://www.smithsonianmag.com/smart-news/watch-winners-2017-dance-your-phd-competition-180967068. Accessed 27 Jan 2019.

---

[29] See Graham Pont, "Plato's Philosophy of Dance" (*Dance, Spectacle, and the Body Politick, 1250–1750*, ed. Jennifer Nevile. Bloomington: Indiana University Press, 2008).

[30] The figure of a dancing Plato has other precedents. In *The Birth of Tragedy*, Nietzsche conjures three figures, Dionysus, Apollo, and Socrates, posing them as gods and instincts. For him, the death of tragedy occurs with Euripides, when the artistic Apollo forsakes the musical Dionysus for the theoretical Socrates. With Wagner, Nietzsche foresaw a new birth of tragedy, which he posed as a music-making Socrates, inspired by the philosopher's own turn to music while awaiting the hemlock *pharmakon*, thus fusing Dionysus with theorist. In the *Epinomis* dialogue attributed to Plato or his school, the Stranger anticipates the Nietzsche of *The Birth of Tragedy*. And then there is *The Gay Science* and Ariadne.

66 J. MCKENZIE

Deleuze, Gilles, and Felix Guattari. 1987. *A Thousand Plateaus: Capitalism and Schizophrenia*. Trans. Brian Massumi. Minneapolis: University of Minnesota Press.

Duarte, Nancy. 2010. *Resonate: Present Visual Stories that Transform Audiences*. Hoboken: Wiley.

Dunne, Anthony, and Fiona Raby. 2007. Critical Design FAQ. Retrieved April 1, 2016, from www.dunneandraby.co.uk/content/bydandr/13/0

Edelman, Jonathan, and Rebecca Currano. 2011. Re-representation: Affordances of Shared Models in Team-Based Design. In *Design Thinking: Understand – Improve – Apply, 61 Understanding Innovation*, ed. Hasso Plattner, Christoph Meinel, and Larry Leifer, 61–79. Berlin/Heidelberg: Springer.

Latour, Bruno. 1986. Visualisation and Cognition: Drawing Things Together. In *Knowledge and Society Studies in the Sociology of Culture Past and Present*, ed. H. Kuklick, vol. 6, 1–40. Greenwich: Jai Press.

LeFever, Lee. 2012. *The Art of Explanation*. Hoboken: Wiley.

McFadden, Tom. 2017. *Science with Tom*. Website. Retrieved January 27, 2019, from https://www.sciencewithtom.com

———. 2018. Science Rap Academy. YouTube. Video playlist. Last updated July 26. https://www.youtube.com/playlist?list=PLvgILFwoRX2min-PEDNXfk2 5KULkKfy7S&app=desktop. Accessed 27 Jan 2019.

McKenzie, Jon. 2013. Smart Media at the University of Wisconsin-Madison. *Enculturation: A Journal of Rhetoric, Writing and Culture* 15. http://www.enculturation.net/smart-media

———. 2016. DesignLab & The Democratization of Digitality. *YouTube*. August 12. TEDxUW-Madison. https://www.youtube.com/watch?v=YmYgTy2VkBU

McLuhan, Marshall, and Quentin Fiore. 1967. *The Medium is the Massage: An Inventory of Effects*. New York: Bantam Books.

Nietzsche, Friedrich. 1993. *The Birth of Tragedy Out of the Spirit of Music*. New York: Penguin.

Olson, Randy. 2015. *Houston. We Have a Narrative: Why Science Needs Story*. Chicago: University of Chicago Press.

Plato. 1928. *The Epinomis of Plato*. Oxford: Clarendon Press.

Pont, Graham. 2008. "Plato's Philosophy of Dance" *Dance, Spectacle, and the Body Politick, 1250–1750*. Ed. Jennifer Nevilel. Bloomington: Indiana University Press.

Rodowick, D.N. 2001. *Reading the Figural, or, Philosophy After New Media*. Durham: Duke University Press.

Rumsey, Abby Smith. 2010. Emerging Genres in Scholarly Communication, Report of Scholarly Communication Institute 8. University of Virginia Library. http://uvasci.org/institutes-2003-2011/SCI-8-Emerging-Genres.pdf

Smith College. 2016. The Design Thinking Initiative. Retrieved May 15, 2016, from http://smith.edu/design-thinking/

StoryCenter. n.d. About StoryCenter. https://www.storycenter.org/about/. Accessed 23 Mar 2018.

Tufte, Edward. 2006. *Beautiful Evidence.* Cheshire: Graphics Press.

University of Wisconsin-Madison. 2016. DesignLab Smart Media. Webpage. designlab.wisc.edu/smart-media. Accessed 7 July 2016.

Wagstaff, Steel. 2012. The{Silence}Project: Some Adventures in Remediation. *Enculturation: A Journal of Rhetoric, Writing and Culture* 15. Published: September 27. http://www.enculturation.net/essays-into-silence-noise-and-john-cage. Accessed 9 July 2018.

Wikipedia contributors. Dance Your PhD. *Wikipedia, The Free Encyclopedia.* Last Modified December 3. https://en.wikipedia.org/wiki/Dance_Your_PhD

Wood, Catherine. 2007. *Yvonne Rainer: The Mind Is a Muscle.* London: Afterall.

CHAPTER 3

Becoming Builder: Generating Collaborative Platforms

Fig. 3.1 KAMG group presentation of reCLAIM Café by Miranda Curry, Aaron Hathaway, Keegan Hasbrook, and Grace Vriezen. University of Wisconsin–Madison. 2016. (Photo by author)

© The Author(s) 2019
J. McKenzie, *Transmedia Knowledge for Liberal Arts and Community Engagement*, Digital Education and Learning, https://doi.org/10.1007/978-3-030-20574-4_3

From Makers to Builders

Wrestling with Plato's Fight Club means grappling with media and also with institutions and oneself. The transformation of the liberal arts from a literate institution to a digital one has been underway for half a century, but still faces many challenges, not only technological and organizational but also cultural. Digital culture is a maker culture, yet the model of making changes dramatically—from individual Romantic genius to that of collective postmodern bricoleurs, makers who collaboratively create with any medium necessary and any means available, often using found, repurposed materials. The Romantic genius remains a powerful model of creativity in liberal arts education, one closely tied to the spaces of seminars (the writer), studios (the artist), and labs (the scientist), as well as and the values of originality and exceptional natural ability. In this model, individual creativity opposes the power of institutions, with power conceived only as repressive and negative, with knowledge serving as the means of liberation. Michel Foucault famously countered this opposition of power and knowledge with knowledge-power: knowledge presupposes power and comes into different arrangements (*dispositifs*). Foucault defines disciplinary power as positive and productive of modern subjects and objects alike.[1] Modern institutions have generated and shaped our very concept of being human—being becomes grounded in human subjects and clear ideas with Descartes—but with the shift from disciplinary to control societies, unified subjects and objects become multiple and intersectional, constructed and deconstructed, looped into each other. Within the transversal space of StudioLab, creativity becomes collaborative and recombinant, mixing not only bodies and media but also pedagogies and infrastructures. The value here is not originality but transformation, even metamorphosis: in StudioLab, students first become makers, then become *builders*, producers of critical design teams that draw on institutional resources to make shared experiences and build collaborative platforms (Fig. 3.1).

Becoming builder entails the self-organization of makers into collective ensembles: critical design teams who research, design, and build both projects and the infrastructure necessary for their collaborative activities, which include organizational structures (production roles, decision-making processes), communication networks (email, Google Docs, websites),

---

[1] See Michel Foucault, *Discipline and Punish* (New York: Vintage Books, 1995).

and micro-cultures (habits, styles, material artifacts, and affective invest-ments). Critical design teams produce transmedia knowledge and come with their own power dynamics, and we can initially understand teams as desiring-machines—a term used by Gilles Deleuze and Felix Guattari to describe small assemblages of bodies and mechanisms which intervene in larger sociotechnical systems, institutions understood as composed of both people and technologies. 'There are no desiring-machines that exist outside the social machines that they form on a large scale; and no social machines without the desiring machines that inhabit them on a small scale.'[2] Research teams, art movements, garage bands, theory schools, start-ups, and activist groups—all constitute desiring-machines that draw on and off larger institutions for discourses and practices and many other resources, even if they set out to break away, resist, or transform them. Power dynamics of class, gender, sexuality, race, ethnicity, ability, age, and raw chemistry inform these desiring-machines, resonating with those of the wider world, for better and for worse. Within the institution of higher education, StudioLab functions as a desiring-machine for building other desiring-machines, critical design teams capable of generating transmedia knowledge and transvaluation of values for diverse audiences, connecting with desiring-machines in other institutions, and thereby transforming the place of higher education in contemporary society. Here, transmedia knowledge becomes tactical media, and desiring-machines morph into collective assemblages of enunciation—platforms for collective thought-action.

Tactical media is a core component of the StudioLab pedagogy because it supplements the medium of phonetic writing on which traditional critical thinking is based while helping to open the field of critical design. Tactical media intervenes in social situations and has a long history, even if the term is relatively new: the banners and posters used by nineteenth-century labor movements, early twentieth-century suffragettes, and mid-century civil rights activists can all be seen as tactical media, as can any media used to contest and resist dominant forms of power. StudioLab's critical design process combines traditional critical thinking with tactical media-making that relies on collective, recombinant creativity, the mixing of desires and skills, materials and processes. Becoming builder means building shared experiences and collaborative platforms on which to make

---

[2] Gilles Deleuze and Felix Guattari, *Anti-Oedipus: Capitalism and Schizophrenia* (Minneapolis: University of Minnesota Press, 1983), 340.

media, while also working on oneself and on institutions, transforming oneself by creating with others, seeking to enter what psychologist Mihaly Csikszentmihalyi calls a *state of flow* or intense concentration. Such experiences of creative immersion resonate with the mimetic enchantment Plato found in Homeric poetry and the plateaus of intensity cyberneticist Gregory Bateson found in Balinese culture.[3]

In critical design teams, these collective experiences of flow are intermittently broken by moments of critical reflection and analysis. These breaks can be especially productive when collaboration sputters due to interpersonal conflicts. Such conflicts often reveal the power dynamics of desiring-machines, thus engaging with them can generate both personal and interpersonal transformation. Importantly, critical breaks also enable teams to respond to feedback from others, such as instructors, other teams, target audiences, and community partners. Such feedback enables critical design teams to fine-tune and sometimes reorient their collaboration.

This transformational rhythm of creative flows and critical breaks channels the onto-historical power of both oral and literate apparatuses and is essential to the democratization of digitality and design in higher education and beyond. Literate education stresses critical thinking: having expelled other media at the beginning, it has had trouble with creative flows both historically and at the level of being: *eidos* is fixed. Collaborative figuration makes ideas flow.

CRITICAL DESIGN 102: BUILDING COLLABORATION

StudioLab's critical design teams are based on industry work as writer and information architect and teaching experience in programs of multimedia, theater and performance studies, and English, as well as workshops given in fields ranging from biomedical science and environmental science to development sociology, labor relations, and engineering. Here we introduce a series of concepts and practices designed to facilitate the shift from maker to builder. To build collaboration, students perform

---

[3] See Mihaly Csikszentmihalyi, *Flow: The Psychology of Optimal Experience* (New York: Harper & Row, 1990), Eric Havelock, *Preface to Plato* (Cambridge, MA: The Belknap Press of Harvard University Press, 1963), and Gregory Bateson, *Steps to an Ecology of Mind* (New York: Ballantine Books, 1972).

3 BECOMING BUILDER: GENERATING COLLABORATIVE PLATFORMS   73

in different modes, those of *teams*, *bands*, and *guilds*, which correspond roughly to the activities of seminar, studio, and lab. As desiring-machines, critical design teams function to transform makers from highly individualistic *bachelor machines* into collaborative *intimate bureaucracies*, where they role-play as critical design consultants, performing such roles as producers, writers, webmasters, and multimedia makers. Through this collaborative role-play, critical design teams build shared experiences and collaborative platforms while learning to mix cultural, technological, and organizational performances and their associated values of efficacy, effectiveness, and efficiency. The chapter concludes by introducing StudioLab's second design frame, User Experience or UX. We begin, however, with another collection of tutor sites, inspirational collaborations for our critical design teams.

Tactical Media: Critical Art Ensemble

In many ways, Critical Art Ensemble (CAE) offers StudioLab the most provocative of tutor collaborations (critical-art.net). Formed in 1987, this artist activist group opened up the realm of electronic civil disobedience with its 1994 manifesto, *The Electronic Disturbance*, published just after the web went public in 1991 and the Mosaic browser began making it popular in 1993. Long before NSA (National Security Agency) cybersurveillance, criminal ransomware, and WikiLeaks whistleblowers, CAE persuasively argued that power had gone virtual and that new modes of civil disobedience were needed. At the same time, they challenged their peers, contending that artists remained too uninterested in digital media, activists too tied to the streets, and programmers too ensconced in the security state for the necessary collaborations to emerge and develop such modes of resistance.[4] By 2000, however, CAE and groups such as the hacktivists Electronic Disturbance Theater, cyberfeminists subRosa, and the anticorporatists eToy had developed and deployed a range of electronic civil disobedience practices. Each group functions as a desiring-machine, and Critical Art Ensemble, in particular, provides the inspiration for StudioLab's critical design teams.

---

[4] See Critical Art Ensemble, *Digital Resistance* (Brooklyn, NY: Autonomedia, 2001).

74   J. MCKENZIE

CAE explicitly counters the model of the individual Romantic genius in their very name and reinscribes the creation of fine art within the production of tactical media, a key component of our critical design process. Tactical media entails transmedia knowledge and vice versa: both constitute transformational forms of knowledge-power designed to produce specific effects with specific audiences. Over three decades, CAE has produced community events, interactive installations, public programming, infographic posters, radio bikes, videos, websites, books, essays, and pamphlets.

> The tactical media practitioner uses any media necessary to meet the demands of the situation. While practitioners may have expertise in a given medium, they do not limit their ventures to the exclusive use of one medium. Whatever media provide the best means for communication and participation in a given situation are the ones that they will use. Specialization does not predetermine action. This is partly why tactical media lends itself to collective efforts, as there is always a need for a differentiated skill base that is best developed through collaboration.[5]

Specialization can sharpen minds to the dullest of points. Transdisciplinary interventions and collaborative problem solving far from discipline open up specialized, ideational thought to hyperlinked syntheses connections far beyond inductive and deductive logic. These syntheses and their transmedia networks produce holistic thought-action figures through Peircean abduction (cognitive leaps) and Ulmerian conduction (associative revelations or flashes).[6] We think-act across different media and fields of experience. In addition to tactical media, CAE provides StudioLab the organizational infrastructure for producing and practicing thought-action in the world.

> For sustained cultural or political practice free of bureaucracy or other types of separating factors, CAE recommends a cellular structure. [...] While size and similarity through political/aesthetic perspective has replicated itself in the group, members do not share a similarity based on skill. Each member's

---

[5] Critical Art Ensemble, *Digital Resistance* (Brooklyn, NY: Autonomedia, 2001), 8.

[6] On abduction, see Robert Sharpe, "Induction, Abduction, and the Evolution of Science." *Transactions of the Charles S. Peirce Society* Vol. 6, No. 1 (Winter, 1970), 17–33. On conduction, see Gregory L. Ulmer, *Teletheory: Grammatology in the Age of Video* (New York and London: Routledge, 1989), 63.

set of skills is unique to the cell. Consequently, in terms of production, solidarity is not based on similarity, but on difference. The parts are interrelated and interdependent.[7]

CAE's model is the artist cell, not the terrorist cell. StudioLab adds to artist cells other tutors, including theory schools, garage bands, start-ups, and so on—small groups of three to five people bound by shared conceptual and aesthetic interests and diversified in technical training and skills.

While CAE has sought to intervene in art and activist traditions, StudioLab focuses on transforming institutions of higher education, in particular the liberal arts, which range from humanities and social sciences to physical and life sciences. CAE was originally formed by graduate students from different fields at Florida State University, and significantly, has targeted economic and scientific issues. CAE's means of self-organization offers StudioLab students a valuable lesson about scale and sustainability: *their own critical design can become independent and sustainable far beyond the particular context in which they emerge.* While this independent sustainability can arise with graduate students, it is the undergraduates—precisely because of their liberal arts requirements—who are the most radically transdisciplinary (even if few realize that their majors are actually disciplines with their own histories). StudioLab provides the space, means, and opportunity for students to collaboratively integrate their cross-campus learning with real-world action both in and out of school.

Scrambling the Alphabet: Google

For StudioLab, Google (google.com) demonstrates the potential of a collaborative college project not only to exist beyond college but also to help scramble the literate infrastructure of schooling itself. Started in 1996 as a research project by Stanford Ph.D. students Larry Page and Sergey Brin, Google has grown from a small start-up in a garage into one of the world's largest multinational corporations. Page's dissertation project to graph the World Wide Web's structure and Brin's experience on the Stanford Digital Library Project (which sought to digitize all books) combined to produce

---

[7] Critical Art Ensemble, *Digital Resistance*, 65.

76   J. MCKENZIE

a revolutionary search engine that has helped transform the very nature of research: both specialists and nonspecialists can use complex algorithms to search innumerable web files and access texts, images, videos, and maps—and do so at any time, from any place with an Internet connection. The model for Google's PageRank was the Science Citation Index, with the index being a powerful literate tool for cataloging textual citations that dates back to medieval times. Google generated an index of the web in a dynamic, scalable fashion. In 1998, when the search engine still sat on Stanford servers, Brin and Page wrote: 'In designing Google, we have considered both the rate of growth of the Web and technological changes. Google is designed to scale well to extremely large data sets.'[8] Since its inception, Brin and Page's collaboration has helped to democratize digitality by bringing information and media to people's fingertips at scales and speeds that continue to amaze. Like Xerox, FedEx, and Photoshop, but far more powerfully, Google is a trademarked proper name that has also become a transitive verb in common usage: 'to google' means to search the web—to research.

Early on, Brin and Page's idealism drove them to disparage search engines funded by advertising. However, once incorporated Google embraced ads, making it hard to live up to its founding ethos, 'Don't be evil.' Since then, Google has come under numerous attacks—including legal contests—for a wide variety of reasons. Criticisms include: its search algorithms are weighted to produce biased results; its ads and digitalization projects contribute to the commercialization of knowledge; its business practices are unfair and monopolistic; its incessant data collection erodes personal privacy and constitutes a profound form of capitalist dataveillance; its collaboration with the NSA demonstrates that it puts state security over individual freedom; and its cultural ethos harbors industry-wide values of sexism and racism. In this light, Google, for many, embodies the observation attributed to social commentator Eric Hoffer: Every great cause begins as a movement, becomes a business, and eventually degenerates into a racket.[9] There is a lesson here for critical design teams.

---

[8] Sergey Brin and Lawrence Page, "The Anatomy of a Large-Scale Hypertextual Web Search Engine." *Computer Networks and ISDN Systems* 30 (1998), 107–117.

[9] Hoffer's actual quote is "What starts out here as a mass movement ends up as a racket, a cult, or a corporation." Eric Hoffer *The Temper of our Time*, (New York: Harper & Row, 1969), 50–51.

In his 2011 book, *The Googlization of Everything: (And Why We Should Worry)*, media scholar Siva Vaidhyanathan shares his own transformation from Google enthusiast to Google skeptic, before setting out a comprehensive critique, less of Google itself, than of 'how we use Google.' He frames the challenge of googlization—the expansion of Google tools and services into ever wider spheres of society—as a 'public failure': 'when Google does something adequately or cheaply in the service of the public, public institutions are relieved of pressure to perform their tasks well.'[10] Vaidhyanathan's primary interest lies in the impact googlization on books, knowledge, and cultural memory. With googlization, he argues, knowledge is becoming fractured, memory filtered by customized algorithms, and encounters with true difference eliminated. Vaidhyanathan offers his own remedy, a proposal for a Human Knowledge Project, in which libraries function as crucial nodes. He also offers his own recombinant mission statement. The Human Knowledge Project

> … would identify a series of policy challenges, infrastructure needs, philosophical insights, and technological challenges with a single goal in mind: to organize the world's information and make it universally accessible. I am sure Google won't mind if we copy its mission statement.[11]

It helps to place Google and Vaidhyanathan's arguments against googlization within the nested onto-historical contexts that inform StudioLab. The public failure Vaidhyanathan describes predates Google and the birth of the web, as public funding for US education began declining with the rise of neoliberal economics in the 1980s and accelerated with the end of the Cold War. The fracturing of knowledge and marginalization of difference, Vaidhyanathan rightly decries, predates Google by millennia. Disciplinary specialization can be traced back through Descartes' *Discourse on Method* to Aristotle's tree-shaped categories; and the marginalization of difference to Aristotle's Law of Identity (A = A). Google and other search algorithms do filter knowledge, and Vaidhyanathan acknowledges that there are no neutral algorithms, yet literacy itself functions as a massive onto-historical filter—with Plato's exclusion of the poets from the Republic, images, music, dance, and other non-written media have been

---

[10] Siva Vaidhyanathan, *The Googlization of Everything: (And Why We Should Worry)*, 2nd ed. (Berkeley: University of California Press, 2011), 6.

[11] Ibid., 204–205.

78   J. MCKENZIE

filtered out of the realm of true, epistemic knowledge, that is, ideation. Western colonialism and universal reason transmediate the world into *logos*, for better and for worse.

Conversely, Vaidhyanathan's arguments against googlization resonate with Plato's arguments *against* writing in *Phaedrus*. There Socrates argues that writing is not 'a potion for remembering, but for reminding' and that it offers, not true understanding but 'discourse [that] roams about everywhere, reaching indiscriminately those with understanding no less than those who have no business with it, and it doesn't know to whom it should speak and to whom it should not.'[12] In short, Vaidhyanathan's own filter is logocentric, as is much of media studies: he uncritically asserts the positive value of books and libraries without also acknowledging the negative effects of literacy's power, and his critique of the emerging digital 'technocracy' fails to recognize that literacy is itself the most powerful technocracy the world has ever known. He asks the right question: 'Are we headed down the path toward a more enlightened age and enriching global economy, or are we approaching a dystopia of social control and surveillance?'[13] StudioLab's answer is *yes*: technology is *pharmakon*, both remedy and poison, whether it functions in the digital, literate, or oral apparatus.

As performance scholar Diana Taylor argues, the literate archive helped radically transform—and in many cases erase—the customs of cultures built on oral repertoires (embodied repositories of gestures, songs, music, and rituals), a process that required centuries of colonial conquest.[14] Likewise, the digital database has been helping transform the knowledge production of archive-based cultures over the past half-century, a period also notably marked by rapid decolonization. For better and for worse, by digitizing archives and research Google is helping to displace the gatekeepers of modern literacy (scholars, librarians, and publishers), just as the archive helped displace the gatekeepers of traditional orality (elders, healers, and rhapsodists). Vaidhyanathan fears that bloggers, Wikipedia, and Google will become the new experts without considering that the remix of *episteme* and *doxa*, scholars and rappers, logocentric and indigenous

---

[12] Plato, *Phaedrus* (Indianapolis, IN: Hackett Publishing Co, 1995), 275a, 275e. As Derrida reminds us in *Disseminations*, Plato argues against the Sophists' writing practices while arguing for the logocentric writing of the soul, whereby writing captures the ideal *Eidos* and translates ideation into dialectical *Logos*.

[13] Vaidhyanathan, *The Googlization of Everything*, 8.

[14] See Diana Taylor, *The Repertoire and the Archive*, (Durham: Duke University Press, 2003).

media is already producing new forms of transmedia knowledge, in which experts and amateurs coexist and collaborate through projects such as Citizen Science, Citizen History, and community-based research where inquiry is informed and guided by community concerns and needs.

As tutor collaboration, Google demonstrates that a desiring-machine can scale into a global sociotechnical system in a relatively short time, producing pharmacological effects: beneficial, malevolent, undecidable. In case of Google, a pair of graduate students built a research engine (Google Search), and their collaboration grew to create many other collaborative platforms, including a filing system (Google Drive), library (Google Books), cartographic systems (Google Maps and Google Earth), citation index (Google Scholar), and its own campus (Googleplex). The widespread adoption of the Google Classroom—comprised of its word processor (Google Doc), email system (Gmail), and laptop (ChromeBook)—by half of the US elementary and secondary schools is creating a generation of googlized students trained for projects like the Human Knowledge Project.[15] The question StudioLab poses: Does higher education have the flexibility and imagination to retool its logocentric superstructure (faculty, curricula, learning spaces, support services), within its digital infrastructure (databases and systems found in content management systems, libraries, email and calendaring, admissions, etc.), thereby empowering this generation of highly collaborative desiring-machines? Remixing the *pharmakon* of orality, literacy, and digitality, StudioLab provides plug-ins for Google Classroom that enable critical design teams to engage the pharmakological powers of googlization.

(Un)masking Discrimination: The Guerrilla Girls

StudioLab's critical design approach brings the power of critical thinking to new contexts via tactical media and transmedia knowledge, which may be digital, analog, or embodied. One of the most successful and provocative collaborations in this regard has been the Guerrilla Girls, a feminist art activist group formed in 1985 in New York City. Using performance art, street protests, masks, posters, infographics, billboards, videos, books, and the World Wide Web, the Guerrilla Girls have targeted different social

---

[15] See, Natasha Singer, "How Google Took Over the Classroom," (*The New York Times.* May 13, 2017).

institutions—particularly in the art world and entertainment industry—for their sexism, racism, and other forms of discrimination. The Guerrilla Girls' work is simple, direct, and effective: in the late 1980s, they plastered New York City's Soho neighborhood with posters presenting the meager number of women artists shown in New York galleries, thereby forcing a public discussion of sexist exhibition practices that helped introduce more diverse artists into the art world. Their trademark tactical media are gorilla masks, which they wear for very specific reasons: to protect their anonymity, to focus on issues rather individuals, to ward off the stereotypical focus on women's beauty, and to provoke audiences with pointed political and social humor. They often appear as four Guerrilla Girls, but the group has a flexible composition:

> Over 55 people have been members over the years, some for weeks, some for decades. Our anonymity keeps the focus on the issues, and away from who we might be. We wear gorilla masks in public and use facts, humor and outrageous visuals to expose gender and ethnic bias as well as corruption in politics, art, film, and pop culture. We undermine the idea of a mainstream narrative by revealing the understory, the subtext, the overlooked, and the downright unfair. We believe in an intersectional feminism that fights discrimination and supports human rights for all people and all genders.[16]

The Guerrilla Girls' gorilla masks offer a singular incarnation of thought-act figures. They are much more than an idea or symbol, as they exist and perform in the world, harboring specific theoretical and practical powers. Rather than static forms, they gather dynamic forces and are animated by the living persons wearing them and interacting in the world by engaging the flow of different social forces, those of gender, sexuality, race, ethnicity, ableism, and class. The ideas do not disappear, however, as much as become elements within thought-action figures that function as a nexus of sometimes disparate yet resonant knowledges and powers: gorillas, guerrillas, girls, grrls, and so on. While ideation strives for emotional distance between clearly defined subjects and objects, thought-action figures embrace what Deleuze and Guattari call the double deterritorialization of human and world, the opening up of modes of becoming-other through the sharing of affective intensities. In the work of the Guerrilla Girls, the power of pointed humor and outrageous visuals is channeled

---

[16] The Guerrilla Girls, "Our Story," https://www.guerrillagirls.com/our-story. Accessed August 11, 2017, 10:13.

3 BECOMING BUILDER: GENERATING COLLABORATIVE PLATFORMS   81

and released through the wearing of gorilla masks which transform recognizable individuals into anonymous warriors, into living thought-action figures who talk the talk and walk the walk in the halls of masculine power—confronting it with what we might call feminine 'maskulinity'. In their book *Bitches, Bimbos and Ballbreakers: The Guerrilla Girls' Illustrated Guide to Female Stereotypes*, the group tackles stereotypes by critically historicizing them and then, reversing and inverting their negative attributes, embracing them:

> If the world is going to call you a Bitch for being ambitious, outspoken, and in control of your own sexuality, why not accept it and be proud? "Bitches of the world unite" Be tough, get what you want, be a real Bitch. But don't let anyone call you one![17]

With the Guerrilla Girls, stereotypes can themselves become empowering thought-action figures. For groups role-playing as critical design teams, this combination of anonymity, collaboration, and critical humor can empower individual students in ways that the lone creative genius simply cannot. By role-playing and wearing the 'mask' of critical design teams, students refunction common organizational processes by creating provocative and often humorous team names, logos, mission statements, and job titles. Becoming builder entails becoming empowered through the parodying and 'mimikry' of established power. In an age of performative inputs and outputs, data must be visualized to become intelligible: those data visualizations wrapped in stories to make sense, and those stories performed before the right audiences to create impact. The Guerrilla Girls' tactical media makes ample use of factual information, often visualized in tables and charts and disseminated on postcards, posters, and billboards using high contrast images, bright, eye-catching colors, and bold, startling headlines. One of their most famous posters reads: 'Do women have to be naked to get into the Met. Museum? Less than 5% of the artists in the Modern Art sections are women, but 85% of the nudes are female.' The image on the poster, which ran on the New York City buses, was Ingres' *La Grande Odalisque* wearing a gorilla mask. In the Guerrilla Girls' hands, iconic high culture artworks can also become thought-action figures.

---

[17] Guerrilla Girls, *Bitches, Bimbos and Ballbreakers: The Guerrilla Girls' Illustrated Guide to Female Stereotypes* (New York: Penguin Books, 2003), 26.

82   J. MCKENZIE

Critical design teams study such collective practices in order to generate their own collection of tactical media and embodied thought-action figures. Students also study the organizational dimension of activists and other groups as means to self-organize and build their own critical design teams. Different tutor groups offer different lessons. Most strikingly, the Guerrilla Girls have described their ensemble as open and at times dysfunctional.

> Over the past ten years, we've come to resemble a large, crazy but caring dysfunctional family. We argue, shout, whine, complain, change our minds and continually threaten to quit if we don't get our way. We work the phone lines between meetings to understand our differing positions. We rarely vote and proceed by consensus most of the time. Some drop out, but eventually most of us come back, after days, months, and sometimes years.[18]

Similar to CAE, the Guerrilla Girls work by a crazy caring consensus: they say 'yes' to collectivist ideas and projects that have been extensively researched and debated. The group thus offers powerful lessons for one of StudioLab's core missions: to inject values of cultural efficacy into systems dominated by technical effectiveness and organizational efficiency.

The democratization of digitality and design encounters intense cultural resistance, as seen in the well-publicized sexism, racism, and xenophobia found in Silicon Valley. However, as argued in a recent study of reasons that workers leave the tech industries, these problems do not originate in tech industries.

> The ongoing debates about whether the lack of diversity is due to a "pipeline problem" or a "tech culture problem" has failed to accurately frame the problem: that there are a complex set of biases and barriers that begin in pre-school and persist through the workplace. These cumulative biases and barriers prevent the tech ecosystem from being more diverse, inclusive, and representative of the United States population as a whole.[19]

In short, the obstacles to democratizing digitality and design are structural and cultural, and as we have seen, the superstructure dimension lags

---

[18] Emily Faxton, "American Ideas in Three Artist Collectives, in Yale National Initiative," https://teachers.yale.edu/curriculum/viewer/initiative_11.03.02_u, accessed March 20, 2018.

[19] Allison Scott, Freada Kapor Klein, and Uriridiakoghene Onovakpuri, *Tech Leavers Study* (Oakland, CA: The Kapor Center for Social Impact, 2017), n.p.

behind the infrastructural dimension, not just in the US but around the world. Just as the Guerrilla Girls have targeted the art and entertainment worlds, StudioLab's critical design teams learn ways to target the sexism, racism, and xenophobia found in the emerging digital apparatus.

Virtual Consultants: The EmerAgency

A fourth tutor for StudioLab's critical design teams is The EmerAgency, a research group that practices a kind of virtual consultancy or Konsultancy. Its twin mottos are 'Problems B Us. And from Basho, this admonition: Not to follow in the footsteps of the masters, but to seek what they sought.'[20] The latter provides a good understanding of StudioLab's relation to tutor texts; the former resonates with StudioLab's goal to help students problem-solve far from their discipline, by mixing expert and common knowledge—although the EmerAgency approaches problem-solving as part of the problem with literate approaches to knowledge: the problem is us, our very attempt to solve or fix the flux of the world with detached, specialized knowledge. Human mastery of the world is limited if not illusionary and has a checkered past, and thus a more humble, holistic, and prudent way is needed. The EmerAgency's virtual consultations work without portfolio: The group develops and proposes unsolicited projects for established organizations, including the National Park Service, the City of Miami, and the State of Florida, projects that reveal the excess or sacrificial dimension (marked with K) of communities and public infra-structures and services, such as tourism, national parks, and disaster relief. An early project was Florida Rushmore, a proposed attraction to increase state tourism by revealing to travelers the abyssal nature of American national identity formation through a holographic Mount Rushmore-like monument placed inside a Florida sinkhole.[21] Such Konsults reconfigure '… disasters as epiphanies, revealing the fatal strategy underlying all possible scenarios. Disasters intimate Limit, Measure, functioning as messages from Technics, the Other Ontology of our machines.'[22] An important lesson for StudioLab's critical design teams is that digital media

---

[20] The EmerAgency website, http://emeragency.electracy.org, accessed Aug. 8, 2017.

[21] See Gregory L. Ulmer, "METAPHORIC ROCKS: A Psychogeography of Tourism and Monumentality." http://users.clas.ufl.edu/glue/Rewired/ulmer.html. Visited August 10, 2017.

[22] The EmerAgency website, http://emeragency.electracy.org, accessed Aug. 8, 2017.

84   J. MCKENZIE

can function both as a means for providing consultation services to the academy, community members, and policymakers *and* as a medium for receiving messages and revelations from the digital apparatus itself. In short, students consult with other humans and are consulted by a Machinic Other—for instance, through patterns generated by random results from Google searches. Learning to prepare for such revelations is key to StudioLab's approach to creativity and innovation through the construction of desiring-machines and thought-action figures.

The EmerAgency is composed of a transdisciplinary team: media theorist Gregory Ulmer, artists Barbara Jo Revelle and John Craig Freeman, and architect William Tilson, all of whom first collaborated together as the Florida Research Ensemble. As with CAE and Google, The EmerAgency collaboration has bootstrapped itself from literate academies to help invent theories and practices for the digital apparatus. Like StudioLab, The EmerAgency explicitly focuses on the displacement of literacy within digitality, which Ulmer has theorized extensively in terms of 'electracy.'

> What are the electrate equivalents of the literate institutional practices and identity formations? … much of the best theorizing of new media and digital technology today neglects the insights of "apparatus": that the Internet is an emerging institution that is to electracy what school was to literacy; that the categorial, logical, and rhetorical practices needed to function natively in this institution have to be invented, and moreover that the invention of an image metaphysics (the equivalent of what Aristotle accomplished for the written word) has its own invention stream, independent of the features of modern recording equipment.[23]

We have seen this neglect of apparatus with Vaidhyanathan's approach to Google. For critical design teams, the challenge lies in intervening in the googlization of the world using digital as well as literate approaches, including both electrate image metaphysics and literate ideational metaphysics. Again, through transmedia knowledge, ideas become figural and pharmakological.

Central to The EmerAgency's image metaphysics is flash reason, which replaces the slow deliberative judgment of the literate world with flashes of deliberative judgment attuned to the instantaneous, real-time pace of digitality/electracy. Such flashes or revelations emerge through a logic of conduction (which supplements induction and deduction), thinking composed

---

[23] The EmerAgency, http://emeragency.electracy.org, accessed Aug. 8, 2017.

of associative patterns that emerge by cycling through different audiovisual discourses, in particular those of Discipline/Career, Community/ History, Pop Culture, and Family (other possible discourses include Religion and the Street).[24] Superimposing these different discourses produces moire-like patterns of thought.

Conductive flash reason is one way StudioLab's critical design teams produce thought-action figures and embrace the power of branding and collectivist icons (whose artifice displaces natural identity and national symbols). From this perspective, we can grasp the Guerrilla Girls' anonymous gorilla masks as a recombinant thought-action figure that flashes forth from the overlaid discourses of art activism, feminism, *Planet of the Apes*, and sisters (indeed, try a Google image search of those four terms). Similarly, through transmedia knowledge, StudioLab's critical design teams produce thought-action figures shared with audiences associated with different discourses, including academics and professionals, community members and policymakers, the general public, and even family and friends. Through their collaborations, students usually find that they can easily discuss the most esoteric of topics with different audiences and are eager to share their projects with family and friends, something rarely done with academic papers. Using flash reason, StudioLab's critical design teams create the circumstances needed to receive revelatory, machinic Konsults and translate them into the thought-action figures of transmedia knowledge.

By role-playing as critical design teams, students enter a transformational space where the creative flow associated with orality mixes with the critical breaks of literacy and where the cycling between different audiovisual discourses produces the flash of electrate identity formation. Ulmer describes this mode of identity in terms of avatars found in gaming, while drawing extensively on the Sanskrit history of this term:

> The argument explores the practical consequences of taking seriously the full potential of this Sanskrit name and tradition. 'Avatar' means 'descent,' referring to the incarnation of a god at a time of crisis. […] The player-avatar relation is associated with the history of practical reason and the virtue of prudence, or good judgment. The proposal is to upgrade prudence from

---

[24] See Gregory L. Ulmer, *Teletheory: Grammatology in the Age of Video* (New York and London: Routledge, 1989).

86   J. MCKENZIE

literacy to electracy. Prudence in practice names the ability to use experience of the past to make decisions in present circumstances leading to good outcomes for the collective order in the future: it is a time logic. [...] Apparatus theory shows that this upgrade involves not only the outline of a new mode of inference, but a new mode of identity as well. Avatar is identified as the site of a new experience motivating a shift in behavior and even of being, both individually and collectively.[25]

The EmerAgency's Konsults and flash reason function as incarnations not of gods or spirits but of a Machinic Other, with 'machinic' understood not simply as technology but along the lines of what Deleuze and Guattari call 'machinic phylum,' an inorganic life that runs through humans and technologies to the earth and cosmos themselves. Electrate avatar is environmental, planetary, and cosmic. For StudioLab, becoming builder in digitality entails becoming other through the universe/university, while avatars function as thought-action figures for doing so.

Teams, Bands, and Guilds

Collaborative problem-solving and digital expression have emerged as valuable forms of participatory maker culture.[26] The four tutor groups above offer different insights and figures for collaboratively combining critical thinking and tactical media at various scales for different ends, including social activism, technological innovation, and transdisciplinary post-ideational thinking. In all four groups, we see the importance of self-organization and project management. Becoming builder entails collaborating both to make media and to generate a social and technical platform—a desiring-machine—with which to do so. StudioLab mixes learning activities found in seminar, studio, and lab, while mapping the CAT design frame on to these spaces to help students analyze and create projects with strong conceptual, aesthetic, and technical elements. From these projects emerge shared experiences and collaborative platforms, the self-organization of transmedia knowledge production. Students become builders by cycling through these learning spaces and performing as teams, bands, and guilds, respectively.

Teams form the basic unit of StudioLab's collaborative activities, and they function to conceive, develop, and create the core conceptual elements of transmedia projects. Teams contain three to five students, and

[25] Gregory L. Ulmer, unpublished proposal for *Avatar Emergency*, n.p.

[26] See Henry Jenkins et al., *Confronting the Challenges of Participatory Culture: Media Education for the 21st Century*, (Cambridge: MIT Press, 2009), 8.

their formation generally occurs around shared interests, although other factors may play a determining role, such as interpersonal relations, differing technical skills, or even chance. Teams may self-select or be organized by instructors. When meeting in a media studio, the assembled teams gather around tables arranged to form a single seminar table with a projection screen and whiteboard or blackboard nearby. As a class, projects are assigned, readings analyzed, examples and tutor materials examined, concepts explored, and questions raised and discussed. Role-playing constitutes a crucial dimension of critical design teams, as it enables individual students to become something bigger than themselves, both imaginatively and practically. Emulating specific tutor groups, critical design teams may give themselves distinctive names, write manifestos and mission statements, create logos and websites, and assign members titles and roles—at times outrageous or parodic, but always functional. As seen with the Guerrilla Girls, these names, logos, and roles have the making of thought-action figures. Teams empower individual students to become builders in mind, body, and technique.

Bands are teams jamming aesthetically: bands perform in studio formation and around their own separate tables, usually covered with books, notes, sketches, and laptops. In bands, roles such as writer, webmaster, photoshopper, and videographer emerge and converge around the design and production of the different forms their transmedia projects will take; for example, graphic essay or illustrated proposal, project website, video demo or trailer, and multimedia presentation. Models for bands include rock bands, rap groups, and jazz and classical quartets, with different members making specific contributions to the overall performance. Within bands, students transmediate their team's conceptual content into aesthetic forms, focusing on their desired impact, their composition and structure in time and space, and the look and feel of individual moments. While the conceptual content tends to remain constant across different smart media, the aesthetic shape and appearance may shift dramatically depending on the audience, desired experience, and technical medium. Bands focus on making media consistent with their overall project plans (Fig. 3.2).

While teams and bands have the same composition when performing their respective conceptual and aesthetic activities, guilds enable individuals from different groups to meet and exchange technical skills related to their specific roles. Just as lead guitarists or DJs gather to share and hone specific techniques, students from different bands meet in guilds to focus on technical skills such as Photoshop, WordPress, InDesign, or SketchUp.

Fig. 3.2 Make a toy experience design exercise. University of Wisconsin–Madison. 2016. (Photo by author)

The classroom enters lab formation, with tables sometimes arranged in rows while students learn software from instructors, Lynda.com, YouTube videos, and especially one another. After honing their skills, guild members then bring them back to their bands and collaborate in transmedia production. In StudioLab, not all students need to learn each relevant software, which minimizes the number of lab training sessions. Alternatively, when students do learn all the project-specific software, they can lend a hand to the lead guild member; they can help out when needed with the production of websites, digital images, presentations, and so on. The key aspect of guilds is that they function as a micro learning community, supporting one another's development of media skills.

Critical design teams become builders by cycling through the conceptual, aesthetic, and technical activities of seminar, studio, and lab; spaces that are typically siloed across campus in widely dispersed departments and colleges. This cycling produces transmedia knowledge, and the interweaving of bodies, materials, and skills constitutes a powerful learning experience, enabling students to problem-solve collaboratively by integrating knowledge and know-how from different disciplines into a rich, coherent project embodied across a suite of transmedia genres. These media forms, in turn, can engage a wide variety of audiences and other potential collaborators: researchers, community members, policymakers, funders, and the general public. By building projects that engage different groups through diverse media, teams reveal how digital rhetoric extends and strengthens the force of traditional composition and rhetoric. In sum, by becoming builder, students generate a social and technical platform on which to build projects that strategically connect different social groups.

CRITICAL DESIGN TEAMS AS INTIMATE BUREAUCRACIES

By focusing on collaboration and role-playing, StudioLab's critical design teams develop students' cultural, technological, and organizational skills. As we have seen, traditional writing classes generate individual critical thinkers, while StudioLab produces both individual makers and collaborative builders. Students learn to collaborate as critical design teams by tackling design problems and exploring solutions beyond those possible for individualized critical thinkers. Thus, StudioLab approaches art activist groups—as well as artisan guilds, theory schools, rap groups, and other start-ups—both as objects of study and as heuristic models for inventing the social practices of digital culture and critical design. Students sometimes extend their tutor groups' focus of action or activism, but most often they head out along new paths, incorporating conceptual, aesthetic, technical, and organizational insights into their own projects and production processes.

Art activist groups such as the Guerrilla Girls, Molleindustria, and the Yes Men can be understood as *intimate bureaucracies*, a term that dj readies/ Craig Saper has coined for modes of 'participatory decentralization.'[27] Intimate bureaucracies enable collective action through common infrastructures such as the streets, the Internet, and other public services. As primary examples, dj readies cites Fluxus art and the Occupy Wall Street political movements and their respective use of the postal service and public parks as creative social media.

---

[27] dj readies, *Intimate Bureaucracies: A Manifesto* (Brooklyn, NY: Punctum Press, 2012), 1.

90   J. MCKENZIE

> These forms of organization represent a paradoxical mix of artisanal production, mass-distribution techniques, and a belief in the democratizing potential of electronic and mechanical reproduction techniques. Borrowing from mass-culture image banks, these intimate bureaucracies play on forms of publicity common in societies of spectacles and public relations. Intimate bureaucracies have no demands, no singular ideology, nor righteous path.[28]

Significantly, dj readies is a pen name (in our terms, a thought-action figure) for media theorist Craig J. Saper, who highlights the paradox of intimate bureaucracies: the impersonal institutions and procedures associated with bureaucracies are detoured or recircuited by artists, activists, and other community members for more singular, intimate ends. Within the context of higher education, colleges and universities—especially public institutions—have themselves long served as common infrastructures, providing access to resources and services through libraries, central IT, and physical spaces. A large part of education involves helping students learn ways to use these and many other infrastructures. However, whereas such learning often remains secondary or tacit in disciplinary training, it becomes central in StudioLab: becoming builder means building the emerging social and technical processes of post-ideational thought-action.

By combining singularity and institutions, intimate bureaucracies also help to formalize the infrastructural dimension of StudioLab's missions to democratize digitality and design and remix performative values. Intimate bureaucracies function as desiring-machines or joyful interactions that enable isolated artistic machines to become full-blown collective assemblages of enunciation, worlds of references and values. StudioLab's critical design teams thus seek to scale up creations of joy across different social planes by constructing heterotopias and other creative spaces that resonate with other social movements. In the terms of design thinking: the creative constraints of human desirability and technical feasibility find sustenance with those of economic or ecological viability, the ability to survive within a given milieu or environment. If design thinking brings the power of creative processes to large organizations, intimate bureaucracies bring the power of large organizations to creative processes. The student body is the site where these circuits intersect.

---

[28] Ibid.

Design Frame 2: UX

Studiolab's second critical design frame, UX or user experience, combines the power of digital rhetoric, transmedia knowledge, and collaborative problem-solving. While CAT focuses on conceptual, aesthetic, and technical traits of smart media works, our UX frame shifts the perspective around to focus on the experience of transmedia knowledge: on the different affects that texts, videos, websites, and other media produce with different stakeholders. UX design emerged from the field of human factors or ergonomics, which focuses on how humans interact with technical systems, and has become central to HCI or human-computer interaction. Yet research that started out focusing on end users ultimately puts their experience at the center—and preferably at the very beginning—of any design process. Today, user experience is a core skill set for designing a remarkably wide range of activities, from interfacing with smartphones to shopping in stores to experiencing large-scale environments such as theme parks and even college campuses, such as the Wisconsin Experience, the Berkeley Summer Experience, and innumerable First-Year Experience programs.

In many ways, UX has become an intimate mechanism of contemporary power and knowledge, operating through human-machine interactions and transmedia storytelling, marketing and branding, patient relations and student affairs—to mention just a few areas of application. In *The Experience Economy: Work Is Theater & Every Business a Stage*, B. Joseph Pine II and James H. Gilmore combine business management with theater and performance studies to argue that theme parks and other experience-based industries exemplify the emergence of a new economic stage. Building on agrarian, industrial, and service economies, the experience economy, they contend, produces and commodifies feelings, hopes, and memories.[29] While Pine and Gilmore laud Disney World as a paradigm of experiential economics, Studiolab's critical design perspective also brings into the frame the artist Banksy's *Dismaland* project. A large-scale collaboration, *Dismaland* detours Disney Land's meticulous UX design to expose other experiences of global performativity: the park is in shambles, the guides are belligerent, Cinderella's stagecoach becomes Princess Diana's car crash, and the lakes are full of oil and dotted with refugee boats.[30]

---

[29] Joseph Pine II and James H. Gilmore, *The Experience Economy: Work Is Theater & Every Business a Stage* (Boston: Harvard Business School Press, 1999).

[30] See Christopher Jobson, "Welcome to Dismaland: A First Look at Banksy's New Art Exhibition Housed Inside a Dystopian Theme Park," *Collosal* web blog. August 20, 2015. Accessed February 22, 2019, https://www.thisiscolossal.com/2015/08/dismaland/.

92   J. MCKENZIE

Disney Land and *Dismaland* each constitute entire worlds of thought-action figures, and together they reveal the scalability and the pharmakological properties of UX design. Our UX frame contains three nested areas of focus, defined and refined over many years:[31]

- *Experience design:* the cognitive, emotional, and visceral impact on the audience
- *Information architecture:* the structure of this experience over time and space
- *Information design:* the look and feel of moment-to-moment experiences

Before defining these three areas more extensively, let us first describe them experientially through the design of a haunted house, whose overall UX design seeks to produce horror and fright. The experience design composes this UX through different components: designing the experience of a haunted house commonly involves building on visitors' expectations, heightening their anticipation, either slowly or immediately, suddenly shocking them silly, and then allowing after-shock relief and recovery—and then designing another fright show around the corner. The information architecture structures these experiences throughout the house: the headless figure appears here, the creepy passageway unfolds here, the room with brains and eyeballs happens here. The information design focuses in to compose discrete experiential moments: the bloody headless figure wearing a dark business suit jumps out of a hidden doorway into a dim vestibule; the pitch-black passageway winds around sharp wooden corners, pulsates with heartbeats and dog growls, and oozes with sticky goo on tattered wallpaper and uneven floors; the gray brains and translucent eyeballs float in bloody bowls in a dirty, garlicy kitchen packed with strange instruments, lit by a flickering, buzzing light bulb. Experience design, information architecture, and information design are nested inside one another, each collaboratively contributing to the overall user experience. A critical design team might embed a history of contemporary horror films into the house, with different guild members responsible for the costumes, sets, and lighting/sound, and the band jamming to compose the scariest possible encounter with Jason, Freddy, and Leatherface. As with the CAT

---

[31] See Jon McKenzie, "Towards a Sociopoetics of Interface Design: etoy, eToys, TOYWAR" (*Strategies: A Journal of Theory, Culture and Politics* 14.1 (2001): 121–38). Other related areas commonly associated within UX include interaction design, visual design, and user testing.

frame, UX can potentially be applied to any experience, from bus rides to birthday parties to conference presentations. The UX frame provides a second set of glasses for analyzing, creating, and evaluating transmedia knowledge. Let us now take a closer look at each UX component.

Experience design refers to the *impact* produced on a given audience, impact that could be cognitive, emotional, or visceral—or a combination of all three. Through this experiential impact flows the aesthetic force of transmedia knowledge. Experience design approaches individual and collective experience as raw material that can be gathered, molded, and shaped, and then directed toward particular ends: experience thus has plasticity and potentiality as well as inertia and lack. Donald Norman, the cognitive scientist cum cognitive engineer who coined the term 'user experience,' argues that people bring cognitive models to any experience. Rather than impose a designer's model—and especially an engineer's model—upon a system, Norman contends that the interactive experience must be informed and shaped by the user's expectations. He recommends making elements visible, using natural mapping to leverage familiar relationships, and providing clear feedback when they interact with the system.[32] Brenda Laurel, a scholar, designer, and entrepreneur, has advocated for using theater as a model for designing human-computer interactions. Since theatre has been using multiple media to design the audiences experience for millennia, Laurel argues that the six elements of Aristotle's *Poetics*—plot, character, thought/theme, diction/language, music/sound effects, and spectacle/visual effects—provide the basis of an effective experience design of digital media.[33] Norman's and Laurel's respective stress on cognitive models and dramatic elements help us see the value of approaching transmedia knowledge via media *genres*: genres are not only families of formal traits but also sets of audience expectations, experiences that audiences expect and project into the future. Knowing these expectations, experience designers can then work with them, shaping experiences that meet, augment, and sometimes confound or mix expectations. The transmedia genre of Dance your Ph.D. combines two sets of experiential expectations that many see as contradictory—viewing modern dance and learning science—just as Bertolt Brecht's epic theatre sought both to entertain and instruct. This mix defines a core affect of transmedia knowledge and digitality more generally.

---

[32] See Donald Norman, *The Design of Everyday Things* (New York: Doubleday, 1990).
[33] See Brenda Laurel, *Computers as Theatre* (Reading, MA: Addison-Wesley, 1991).

Information architecture focuses on the *structure* of experiences, the way that multisensory information, materials, and interactions are organized and presented over time and space to create specific experiences. Experience is plastic, and information architecture helps to bend and shape experiences at large scale. Richard Saul Wurman, who first introduced the term 'information architect' (and founded TED talks), argues that information can be organized in five distinct ways: by Location, Alphabet, Time, Category, and Hierarchy. Using location, information architects shape experience spatially or geographically: for instance, clothing stores often place new items up front, sale items in the back, and the checkout counter in the middle. Travelogues often organize information geographically. Libraries organize books alphabetically, first by call numbers and then by author names; a book's index organizes subject topics the same way. History museums often organize their exhibitions chronologically, structuring visitors' experience by decades, centuries, even millennia; history books do so with events. Universities organize their campuses by categories, clustering different disciplines in colleges: arts and sciences, agriculture, engineering, business, medicine, and so on; their websites follow suit. Other organizations typically structure their workers hierarchically, with executive management, directors, team leaders, and team members occupying different spaces; organizational charts depict this hierarchy accordingly. In addition to Wurman's LATCH, experiences can be organized around Analogy (e.g., using a computer's *desktop*), Number (e.g., 'remember these 3 things'), and Acronym (e.g., LATCH or ANALATCH). As we saw with Duarte's sparkline, effective presentations often combine personal narrative (Time) and conceptual logic (Category), which demonstrates a more general point: all of these information architectures can be embedded in one another. A geology book can be organized by chapters on geological periods, subdivided into sections on geographical locations, then into paragraphs using categories, and the entire text wrapped up in a metaphorical title that can appear thematically throughout the book: *Spaceship Earth*, *The Pale Blue Dot*, and so on.

The third element of the UX frame, information design, refers to the *look and feel* of specific moments within the overall experience: the images, texts, sounds, colors, textures, and even smells of a particular webpage, chapter, room, scene, and so on. There is no UX without information design, as even a blank page, total darkness, silence, or white noise produces an experience. Given the dominance of visual perception, information design is often understood as visual or graphic design, in part because of the pioneering work of Edward Tufte. Tufte's self-published books, especially *Envisioning Information*, combine exquisite writing and examples to demonstrate powerful techniques of information design. For instance, small multiples of images or graphs enable viewers to compare differences and similarities quickly. Skillful juxtaposition of scale allows one to grasp micro/macro relations. Fields of muted colors and thin grid lines punctuated with intensely colored points focus attention on crucial data and allow designers to layer and separate information, best exemplified in well-designed maps. Tufte's goal to escape the flatland of the page comes from his lengthy experience with print, and his focus on telling visual narratives with information embodies his ethos of presenting substantive content simply and elegantly. A provocative counterpoint to Tufte's somber, minimalist style can be found in David McCandless's *Information is Beautiful*. Like Tufte, McCandless prioritizes effective visualization of content, but his approach and sensibility produce strikingly different effects. Seeking to contextualize information, he juxtaposes relevant and surprising comparative data, such as the annual carbon footprints (in tons), of heating the average home (1.49), breathing (0.57), and one ton of beef (16), all represented with proportionally sized icons. Such juxtapositions produce revealing patterns of phenomena, dramatized by bright colors and striking uses of font styles. McCandless employs a pop sense of beauty and playful meta-perspectives, such as displaying his book's organization in different ways, depicting different types of visualizations in a table, and charting the year-long process of writing his book in terms of emails, emotional state sequencer, doubt tracker, and the formation of ideas.

Visual design is crucial to information design but sound design, tactical and haptic design, interactive design, even smell and taste can contribute to the overall user experience. A Catholic Mass, for instance, includes visual elements such as the crucifix and clerical garments; the sounds of the spoken liturgy, prayers, and music; the bodily movements of sitting, kneeling, standing, and approaching the altar; the smells of incense; and of course, the eating of consecrated bread and wine delivered by the clergy. The function of the Mass, like the experience design of many rituals in other cultures, entails transporting participants from a profane to a sacred space and back again, and such rituals typically involve a precise set of performances enacted in a particular temporal sequence and spatial structure using a prescribed set of materials and objects.

Experience design, information architecture, and information design are entangled within one another, and together create the overall user

96   J. MCKENZIE

experience. One can start anywhere, but UX design commonly begins with experience design, although a structure or discrete sound can trigger the process. Students occasionally have trouble untangling these areas at first, but we have found that carefully analyzing the impact, structure, and look and feel of the user experience of different but closely related media forms *and then having them make their own suites of transmedia knowledge* helps them to do so. To teach UX: define, demonstrate, and get out of the way.

STEEL, CAGE, AND REDESIGNING SILENCE

We can further distinguish the components of the UX frame by reanalyzing Steel Wagstaff's seminar paper, graphic essay, and video essay. As we saw using the CAT frame, the conceptual content remains largely constant across all three transmediations, while the aesthetic and technical aspects vary considerably. The UX frame reveals that the experience design—the intended impact—of the three works differ despite having the same conceptual content. The seminar paper primarily seeks to persuade readers of Cage's innovative approach to music, sound, and silence using argumentative logic and textual description and citation while establishing a distance between the analysis and its object. This critical distance is a defining power and affect of the literate technology of Plato's Fight Club: stop the music and analyze it. Wagstaff, however, also plays with this distance through a reflective writing style that brings footnotes and parenthetical remarks to the foreground, bringing the reader into a more intimate relationship with the scholarly apparatus.

The graphic essay transmediation creates a highly demonstrative, highly visual impact by adding images that both illustrate and supplement Wagstaff's argument, evoking additional associations, introducing nonlinear reading paths, and bringing the reader closer to both Cage and Wagstaff by visually blurring the boundaries of art and life, theory and practice. The video essay in turn brings the viewer/listener even closer to Cage and Wagstaff through the montage of moving images and narration over a rich sonic landscape, heightening the emotional impact and conceptual complexity. Interestingly, the underlying information architecture of Wagstaff's seminar paper, graphic essay, and video essay are consistent: the user experience is divided into three movements, each with its own section title. However, this structure takes on added dimensions with the addition, first, of an image track added to the written text in the graphic essay, and then with the video essay, a narrated moving image track with textual script, music and other sonic elements. If the original seminar paper provided the specifications of a building, the graphic essay adds full-color and a punk-style 2D rendering, and the video essay a pulsating, 3D fly-through. This transformation of experience design and information architecture occurs moment by moment at the micro-level of information design. The seminar paper's single-sided, 8.5×1-inch white paper with black 12-point serif font and 1-inch margins becomes transmediated into double-sided, two-page spreads with full-bleeds (ink printed to the paper's edge), single and double columns of text, headlines and callouts, multiple fonts in different colors, as well as photographs of Cage, street signs, buildings, people signaling 'silence' with a finger over their mouth, and a closing image of Wagstaff. By introducing his body, his experience, his voice into the flow of transmediation, Wagstaff accomplishes the collapse of literate critical distance and the Fluxus breakdown of the art/life divide. Indeed, he embodies Cage's neoDada aesthetics with his own aesthetic choices, applying Cage's open-ended chance operations to his own cultural context.

We see and hear this steely Cagean blend most strongly in the video essay, where alongside the music and images of Cage, we find both historical and contemporary materials reflective of Wagstaff's own experience and tastes, including music clips from The Big Bopper, The Beatles, Bjork, and many others; all mixed together in an extraordinary sound design that rhythmically rhapsodizes a theory of Cage's music. If Plato's Fight Club stopped the music, StudioLab helps to restart it. Recalling Nietzsche's evocation of a 'music-making Socrates,' transmedia knowledge entails theory set to music—or theory produced through music. From text to graphic essay to video essay, Wagstaff transmediates the Cagean experience of silence, and in the video essay returns it to the medium of sound: we hear Cage speak, hear *3′44″* performed, and hear the silence around us.

The UX frame provides critical design teams a robust formal language for analyzing potentially any work of knowledge, cultural expression, or everyday life situation: for example, describe the UX of a favorite class, a party, or a work environment. As importantly, UX enables teams to design transmedia knowledge projects that seek to produce specific effects for different audiences—peers, community members, policymakers, and so on. It also empowers them to evaluate the efficacy of their work: for example, does this seminar paper, public presentation, or online video create the impact it seeks to produce? Finally, UX provides students with a valuable set of concepts and skills crucial to a wide variety of fields, including engineering, computer science, industrial design, marketing, and through

98   J. MCKENZIE

design thinking (as we will see in the next chapter), also management, social activism, and community-based research. Indeed, UX design, experience design, information architecture, and information design are each now career tracks. In its mission to democratize digitality by democratizing design, StudioLab seeks to refunction UX within the context of higher education to help transform the liberal arts.

EVALUATING COLLABORATIVE PLATFORMS

StudioLab's design frames address some of the most pressing challenges facing twenty-first-century higher education: how to assess 'born digital' student work, how to translate materials across emerging scholarly genres, and how to evaluate transmedia knowledge and collaborative academic projects? These frames can be combined in different ways, and here we extend CAT to evaluate the UX within critical design teams, that is, the students' own experience of collaboration. The different transmedia forms and the CAT design frame's conceptual, aesthetic, and technical components provide a first language to describe, analyze, create, and evaluate digital work, emerging scholarly genres, and transmedia knowledge. The CAT frame, however, can also be extended to enable both faculty and students to describe and assess the collaborative dimension of projects, the UX of critical design teams. By adding an O for organization, CAT becomes CATO, and collaboration emerges as part of the extended design frame. Self-organizing as critical design teams and role-playing within them, students perform specific roles and undertake assigned tasks, typically as writers, graphic designers, website designers, and producers. Students generally enjoy giving themselves playful titles and serious roles, as the formation of teams, bands, and guilds is explicitly framed as a collaborative RPG, a role-playing game. Part of the game's equipment is the CATO frame, which both the instructor and students use to oversee and evaluate the conceptual, aesthetic, technical, and organizational performance of team members. In many ways, the O helps everyone take care of the CAT—the organizational integration of conceptual, aesthetic, and technical dimensions; the relation between seminar, studio, and lab activities, and the accompanying circulation between team, band, and guild.

The O encompasses the organization, communication, and evaluation of collaborative and individual work within the intimate bureaucracy of the team. The Guerrilla Girls' self-description as a dysfunctional family points to both the joyful and painful potential of any collaborative project.

When groups enter into flow, collaborators' individual creative and critical energies converge seamlessly, and participants experience communal joy while undertaking even the most taxing of work—indeed, work becomes play. A space emerges, a collaborative platform, the desiring-machine's experiential architecture. Yet, as most everyone has experienced, collaboration can also become difficult, painful, and sometimes even hellish. Intimacy can be intimidating. Tensions can arise over the group or project's very definition and desired impact, over aesthetic decisions or technical execution, over contributions of individual team members, over scheduling, you name it. In addition to time management and workflow problems, we often see issues of gender come to the fore as male and female members display sexist attitudes toward each other. Racial and ethnic differences can also arise, as well as issues of ableism. And sometimes, interpersonal chemistries can become corrosive and even explosive. In all of these cases, individuals' creative and critical energies begin to diverge, and the desiring-machine can enter a black hole. Such tensions mirror those found in other collaborative contexts and in social situations at large. And incredibly, good and even great work is sometimes produced.

Rather than viewing these challenging, divergent energies as reasons to avoid collaboration, StudioLab approaches them as opportunities for critical discussion and creative syntheses. Unless these tensions are addressed, students can harbor frustrations around fairness and accountability that negatively affect their overall learning experience. Organizational performance entails sharing information and decision-making about group and project priorities, defining individual responsibilities, respecting different perspectives and skill levels, communicating work progress in a timely fashion, meeting project deadlines, and attending class and out-of-class meetings, and fulfilling group expectations and individual responsibilities. Instructors can get some sense of a group's organizational performance through observation and discussion, although sometimes groups prefer not to share emergent frustrations openly, often out of concern about grades or simply because they believe it is inappropriate due to the academic context. At other times, however, a student or two may approach instructors with issues about the group's overall workflow or a particular member not meeting their responsibilities. Here instructors become facilitators, meeting with the group to encourage better communication of expectations and responsibilities and, when appropriate, discuss the situation and seek a way forward. Here we can see issues of cultural efficacy, technical effectiveness, and organizational efficiency.

The most important aspect of CATO involves foregrounding the power dynamics of transmedia knowledge production by decentering the evaluative process to include both instructor and students. To this end, students evaluate their own group members' organizational performances, how well each individual contributes to the project, meets the group's self-defined expectations, and fulfills individual responsibilities. Thus, in addition to asking students to evaluate all group project presentations using CAT, we also ask each student to describe and assess their own group members' individual organizational performance using CATO: what were the individual responsibilities, and how well did each group member contribute to the conceptual, aesthetic, technical, and organizational success of the project? Once a major project is completed and turned in, students email their CAT and CATO evaluations to instructors, and these evaluations help inform the grading process, along with the group's transmedia (e.g., graphic essay, presentation media, website) and instructor observation.

By decentering the evaluative process and foregrounding the power dynamics within transmedia knowledge production, StudioLab enables students to think and act critically about their own work and the institutional role of performance evaluation in contemporary society. Further, as intimate bureaucracies begin working with other partners, such as community organizations, nonprofits, and local businesses, they encounter the evaluative frameworks and power setups at work in other collaborative platforms. It is by engaging these different frameworks that shared experiences of transmedia knowledge make possible the transvaluation of performative values.

EXPERIENTIAL ARCHITECTURES AND COLLECTIVE THOUGHT-ACTION

Becoming builder entails making shared experiences of transmedia knowledge as well as crafting the collaborative platforms through which to do so. The UX design frame extends beyond the impact of transmedia knowledge and into the social and technical aspects of creativity and critique, which are ignored by definition with the figural *dispositif* of the Romantic genius, who suffers isolation and misunderstanding while raging against society and the machine. Today, we recognize how constructed this thought-action figure has become, and also how powerful it remains: the tortured artist, the mad scientist, the crazy entrepreneur—each is alive if not well, walking and talking all around us. But through this constructedness and survival, we can also recognize the sociotechnical systems that help produce and maintain this figure: popular culture, high culture, institutions such as education, business, journalism, and the Great Man version of history. We also recognize how the politics of gender, race, class, and species have shaped, and now challenge, its composition.

The figure of the Romantic genius, in short, is the product of modern, disciplinary design, and while the structure and details of its UX vary widely, historically, its dominant representation and experience design has been one of isolated suffering. By contrast, the postmodern UX of critical design teams—modeled on artist cells, rock bands, and start-ups—projects like a beacon the shared experience of joy, flow, and becoming. This is not to say that the Romantic genius does not produce joy: indeed, ecstatic, revelatory experiences of nature, the universe, or the sublime commonly characterize this figure. Nor is collaboration free from suffering and pain, individual or collective, far from it. Lots of bands and movements go into black holes. Yet these two figures emerged on different onto-historical strata with different societies and institutions, and today, they perform in anachronistic juxtaposition.

The formation of critical design teams entails shared experiences that produce platforms of intensity, interaction, trust, and communication—all unfolding in a common critico-creative project. We call such platforms *experiential architectures* to stress that the production of transmedia knowledge occurs not only across physical and digital spaces but also across experiential ones—and that the connection between these spaces is itself transmediated. In many ways, experiential architectures self-organize a team's inner workings, its desiring-machinations, and yet they simultaneously emerge in contact with an environmental milieu and an outside. Experiential architectures are shared platforms of transmedia knowledge common to both experimental desiring-machines and highly normative sociotechnical systems; they are what enable intimate bureaucracies to detour institutional flows and, alternatively, allow institutions to mine and appropriate mutant experiments. If we cast thought-action figures as dynamic or even chaotic systems, then experiential architectures are their surrounding environments, their uncanny homes. Philosophical systems, sacred cosmographies, secret societies, Facebook groups, college campuses, community centers, city streets, intimate bureaucracies—all constitute

102   J. MCKENZIE

homes or ecologies of collective thought-action. All constitute experiential architectures, small and large.

Critical design teams make thought-action figures and build the experiential architectures that support and house them. Experiential architectures enable the scalability and sustainability of transmedia knowledge and performative transvaluations, both within critical design teams and in their engagement with others. The experience of building platforms for collective thought-action radiates outward from teams to partners and stakeholders, whether these be peers, communities, policymakers, general public, and so on. Once again, the collaborative production of tactical media and protest events by activist groups provide important lessons here. In its early years, ACT-UP member Jon Greenberg connected the external goal of the group's demonstrations—to force their targets to change AIDS-related health policies—to their internal goal: the transformation of anger and fear within ACT-UP members themselves.

> Anger is not empowerment. Knowledge is empowerment. But the anger has to be released (sometimes a lot of it, for a long time) before we can allow the knowledge to flow as freely as it should. ACT UP demonstrations are primal scream therapy for people who would never voluntarily engage in primal scream therapy. Get the anger out so we can open up to love, knowledge and power.[34]

Demonstrations are shared transmedia experiences: through signs and banners, songs and marches, media disturbances and public protests, ACT-UP connects the group's collaborative platform—its experiential architecture of anger and love, knowledge and power—with others, in order to gain empathy with hospitals and pharmaceutical companies, politicians and policymakers, the media and the general public. ACT-UP explicitly draws on the civil disobedience tradition of Gandhi and King, whose collective actions likewise entailed transforming anger and fear into love, knowledge, and empowerment. Through such experiential architectures, the shared UX of collective thought-action comes into focus, and we can better understand the experience design of becoming maker, becoming builder, and becoming cosmographer. One works on oneself in a collaborative team with larger communities.

---

[34] Jon Greenberg, "ACT UP Explained" www.actupny.org/documents/greenbergAU. html, accessed November 19, 2018.

What Could Be: A Thousand Platos

To democratize digitality, StudioLab seeks to democratize design, which entails not just becoming maker of transmedia knowledge but also becoming builder of collaborative platforms. Critical thinking becomes critical design through collective thought-action, extending students' experiential architectures out into the field. In *A Thousand Plateaus*, Deleuze and Guattari speak of a plane of consistency composed of 'assemblages capable of plugging into desire, of effectively taking charge of desires, of assuring their continuous connections and transversal tie-ins.'[35] Critical design teams' collaborative experiences generate such planes of consistency; first, as students role-play and self-organize into intimate bureaucracies with roles and brands, projects and production processes—as makers become builders—and then second, as these intimate bureaucracies begin interacting with other teams and eventually with different partners and stakeholders—that is, as builders start to become cosmographers or co-designers of worlds. Planes of consistency enable desiring-machines' collaborative platforms to scale and survive, and while the CAT and UX design frames facilitate these transformations of the student body, StudioLab's plane of consistency really takes off with the DT frame, which assigns shared media a generative role within its post-ideational design process while prioritizing the place of human desirability.

Desire has a long history in Plato's Fight Club and includes both sexual and community relations. From our perspective, the Academy started as out as a small desiring-machine whose experiential architecture consisted of columns and gardens as well as symposia, texts, and temperaments. Sloterdijk asserts that Plato established the Academy to get the gadfly Socrates off the streets and into a safe place.[36] Within the Fight Club, Plato and crew wrestled with poetry and sophistry and also with wrestling itself, the homosocial, pederastic traditions of Archaic and Classical Greece. Plato's Fight Club famously countered this erotic love with another all-too-male intimacy; the Academy espoused what would become known as Platonic love, *philo-sophia,* the love of wisdom, defined as the knowledge of ideal forms—*eidos.* Extending this strange new desiring-machine and its experiential architecture back out into the world and constructing a plane

---

[35] Gilles Deleuze and Felix Guattari, *A Thousand Plateaus* (Minneapolis: University of Minnesota Press, 1987), 166.

[36] See Peter Sloterdijk, *Critique of Cynical Reason* (Minneapolis: University of Minnesota Press, 2008).

104   J. MCKENZIE

of consistency there would prove both rewarding and costly—and would extend far beyond the lives of these early academicians. The rockiness of the Fight Club's community engagement in Athens has likewise become famous—and infamous—through the trial and death of Socrates, but nevertheless its plane would prove to be both scalable and sustainable for millennia. Plato's Academy survived for centuries in Greece and later became a paradigm of universal reason replicated around the world. Today, there are over 26,000 universities worldwide, a global network of Fight Clubs, many arrayed with white columns and campus gardens, all hosting symposia. This experiential architecture remained an almost exclusively phallocentric affair well into the twentieth century.

Thus, along the way, indeed from the very start, the Platonic plane of consistency harbored what Deleuze and Guattari call a plane of organization, a second plane which 'concerns the development of forms and the formation of subjects.'[37] Their notion of Body without Organs, borrowed from Antonin Artaud, deterritorializes this plane of organization into the plane of consistency, while Organs without Bodies territorialize its flows into forms. Indeed, such a plane of organization constitutes a defining feature of Platonic thought, which adds a plane of transcendent, ideational forms over the world ($n + 1$), while the plane of consistency extends itself immanently, its multiplicities subtracting the unity of forms and subjects into flows of intensity ($n - 1$).[38] One event happened over there-then; the other unfolds here-now. As intimated earlier, for critical design teams, experiential architectures connect their desiring-machines with sociotechnical systems. These collaborative platforms are also places where the planes of consistency and organization encounter one another—and do so through transmedia knowledge and collective thought-action. Like transmedia knowledge, collaborative platforms are pharmakological, undecidable, able to pass into planes of consistency or organization. This multivalency is both the risk and the chance of intimate bureaucracies as they become cosmographic.

To draw together this book's experiential architecture and extend it outward: broadly speaking, Plato, collaborative platforms, and planes of consistency all compose a *plateau* that stretches back through English, Spanish, French, and Latin worlds to the Greek word *platus*—'broad.' But why stop in this place?

---

[37] Ibid., 265.
[38] Ibid., 21.

3 BECOMING BUILDER: GENERATING COLLABORATIVE PLATFORMS   105

We call a 'plateau' any multiplicity connected to other multiplicities by superficial underground stems in such a way as to form or extend a rhizome. We are writing this book as a rhizome. It is composed of plateaus. We have given it a circular form, but only for laughs.[39]

Play, too, plays its part on our Platonic plateau: *play*, from the Old English *pleg(i)an* 'to exercise', *plega* 'brisk movement', related to Middle Dutch *pleien* 'to leap for joy, dance.' Dancing Plato as joyful multiplicity: a thousand Platos playing on twenty-six thousand plateaus with platters and plates, places and plans all up in the air—everything cascading across different media forms and collaborative platforms, nothing taking place but the place. Often dismissed within ideational knowledge as word-play, visual puns, or mere coincidence, such plateaus *make another sense possible* in transmedia knowledge, the sense of collective thought-action figuration, which resonates here and there with philharmonic orchestras and techno raves, *feng shui* and dream time. On this plateau, the tree experiences the rhizome as contagion, and contagion it is. Artaud, a maker of plays, poems, drawings, theory, and radio, tunes us into all this from beyond:

The plague takes images that are dormant, a latent disorder, and suddenly extends them into the most extreme gestures; the theater also takes gestures and pushes them as far as they will go: like the plague it reforges the chain between what is and what is not, between the virtuality of the possible and what already exists in materialized nature.[40]

Shuttling between what is and what is not, between factuals and counterfactuals, what is and what could be, critical design teams build experiential architectures for generating other possible worlds. The plateau of the field awaits.

REFERENCES

Artaud, Antonin. 1958. *The Theater and Its Double*. Trans. Mary Caroline Richards. New York: Grove Press.
Bateson, Gregory. 1972. *Steps to an Ecology of Mind*. New York: Ballantine Books.
Brin, Sergey, and Lawrence Page. 1998. The Anatomy of a Large-Scale Hypertextual Web Search Engine. *Computer Networks and ISDN Systems* 30: 107–117.
Critical Art Ensemble. 1994. *The Electronic Disturbance*. Brooklyn: Autonomedia.

[39] Ibid., 2.
[40] Antonin Artaud, *The Theater and Its Double* (New York: Grove Press), 27.

106   J. MCKENZIE

———. 2001. *Digital Resistance: Explorations in Tactical Media*. Brooklyn: Autonomedia.

Csikszentmihalyi, Mihaly. 1990. *Flow: The Psychology of Optimal Experience*. New York: Harper & Row.

Deleuze, Gilles, and Felix Guattari. 1983. *Anti-Oedipus: Capitalism and Schizophrenia*. Trans Robert Hurley, Mark Seem, and Helen R. Lane. Minneapolis: University of Minnesota Press.

———. 1987. *A Thousand Plateaus: Capitalism and Schizophrenia*. Trans. Brian Massumi. Minneapolis: University of Minnesota Press.

Derrida, Jacques. 1981. *Dissemination*. Trans. Barbara Johnson. Chicago: University Press.

dj readies. 2012. *Intimate Bureaucracies: A Manifesto*. Brooklyn: Punctum Press.

EmerAgency. n.d. Welcome. Website. http://emeragency.electracy.org. Accessed 8 Aug 2017.

Faxton, Faxton. 2002. *American Ideas in Three Artist Collectives, in Yale National Initiative*. https://teachers.yale.edu/curriculum/viewer/initiative_

Foucault, Michel. 1995. *Discipline and Punish: The Birth of the Prison*. New York: Vintage Books.

Greenberg, Jon. 1992. ACT UP Explained. www.actupny.org/documents/greenbergAU.html

Guerrilla Girls. 2003. *Bitches, Bimbos and Ballbreakers: The Guerrilla Girls' Illustrated Guide to Female Stereotypes*. New York: Penguin Books.

———. *Our Story*. Website. https://www.guerrillagirls.com/our-story. Accessed 11 Aug 2017, 10:13.

Havelock, Eric Alfred. 1963. *Preface to Plato*. Cambridge, MA: The Belknap Press of Harvard University Press.

Hoffer, Eric. 1967. *The Temper of Our Time*. New York: Harper & Row.

Jenkins, Henry, with Ravi Puroshotma, Katherine Clinton, Margaret Weigel, and Alice J. Robison. 2009. *Confronting the Challenges of Participatory Culture: Media Education for the 21st Century*. Cambridge, MA: MIT Press.

Jobson, Christopher. 2015. Welcome to Dismaland: A First Look at Banksy's New Art Exhibition Housed Inside a Dystopian Theme Park. *Collosal web blog*, August 20. https://www.thisiscolossal.com/2015/08/dismaland/. Accessed 22 Feb 2019.

Laurel, Brenda. 1991. *Computers as Theatre*. Reading: Addison-Wesley.

McKenzie, Jon. 2001. Towards a Sociopoetics of Interface Design: etoy, eToys, and TOYWAR. *Strategies: A Journal of Theory, Culture and Politics* 14 (1): 121–138.

Norman, Donald. 1990. *The Design of Everyday Things*. New York: Doubleday.

Pine, Joseph, II, and James H. Gilmore. 1999. *The Experience Economy: Work Is Theater & Every Business a Stage*. Boston: Harvard Business School Press.

Plato. 1995. *Phaedrus*. Trans. Alexander Nehamas and Paul Woodruff. Indianapolis: Hackett Publishing Co.

Scott, Allison, Freada Kapor Klein, and Uriridiakoghene Onovakpuri. 2017. *Tech Leavers Study*. Oakland: The Kapor Center for Social Impact.

Sharpe, Robert. 1970. Induction, Abduction, and the Evolution of Science. *Transactions of the Charles S. Peirce Society* 6 (1): 17–33.

Singer, Natasha. 2017. How Google Took Over the Classroom. *The New York Times*, May 13. https://www.nytimes.com/2017/05/13/technology/google-education-chromebooks-schools.html. Accessed 14 June 2017.

Taylor, Diana. 2003. *The Repertoire and the Archive*. Durham: Duke University Press.

Ulmer, Gregory L. 1989. *Teletheory: Grammatology in the Age of Video*. New York/London: Routledge.

———. 2017. Metaphoric Rocks: A Psychogeography of Tourism and Monumentality. http://users.clas.ufl.edu/glue/Rewired/ulmer.html. Accessed Aug 10.

Vaidhyanathan, Siva. 2011. *The Googlization of Everything: (And Why We Should Worry)*. Berkeley: University of California Press.

CHAPTER 4

Becoming Cosmographer: Co-designing Worlds

Fig. 4.1 Screen grab from Art of Transformation demo, created in MapTu by researchers in UMBC's Imaging Research Center to visualize interview content and project feedback of Baltimore community members. The University of Maryland–Baltimore County. (Image by IRC)

© The Author(s) 2019
J. McKenzie, *Transmedia Knowledge for Liberal Arts and Community Engagement*, Digital Education and Learning, https://doi.org/10.1007/978-3-030-20574-4_4

110 J. MCKENZIE

FROM BUILDERS TO COSMOGRAPHERS

In many ways, the challenge facing the liberal arts may come down to a spatial one, as over the centuries Plato's Fight Club has built itself some very high walls, both inside and out. Lately, it has been losing battles in the public sphere at an alarming rate. Redesigning the academy's relationship with the outside requires reworking the inside, the spaces and activities we use to produce, communicate, and use knowledge. StudioLab generates transmedia knowledge by integrating activities and learning spaces traditionally siloed inside different parts of campus: the seminar activities found in humanities and social sciences, the studio activities found in art and design, and the lab activities found in science and engineering.

Within the StudioLab pedagogy, *becoming maker supplements critical thinking with critical design*, conducting writing through a wider nexus of transmedia while mixing argument and story, idea and image, and *episteme* and *doxa*. The CAT or Conceptual/Aesthetic/Technical design frame provides faculty and students with a formal language for creating and analyzing transmedia knowledge across different scholarly genres. *Becoming builder, in turn, transforms the model of making from Romantic genius to recombinant bricoleur, creator of shared experiences, and collaborative platforms.* Through the formation of critical design teams modeled on activist groups, rock bands, and start-ups, students' role-playing ensemble work interweaves and intensifies their conceptual, aesthetic, and technical skills and enables teams to produce more nuanced and scalable forms of transmedia knowledge. The UX or user experience design frame of experience design, information architecture, and information design helps teams create tactical media campaigns that produce different experiences for different stakeholders while also allowing them to reflect on their own learning experience.

StudioLab's full potential as a critical design practice unfolds in the third transformation it offers: *becoming cosmographer or co-designer of worlds*. Here making and building unfold in a fourth space, that of the field. The field smooths away many of the differences between seminar, studio and lab spaces, for it is their common outside, the space outside discipline and the university, the field of community engagement, of *doxa*. This field ranges from local to distant communities, natural habitats to contested borders, and policy boards and businesses to NGOs and other nonprofit organizations. Within the field, *transmedia knowledge takes on the role of civic discourse*, as communities have long used reports, posters, murals, and media events to advocate for recognition and action within their larger community. Becoming cosmographer thus reveals another dimension of critical design, one that extends both media-making and collaborative building into the public sphere: critical design here entails human-centered design focused on social and organizational problems, opening up the critico-creative process to different audiences and other stakeholders—for what is being created in the field are precisely worlds and spheres of complex social life where the stakes are very real, very constraining, and usually themselves in play.

In becoming cosmographer we find the deeper stakes of mixing *episteme* and *doxa*: problem-solving (and/or trouble making) may occur far from one's discipline, for the solution (and/or trouble) emerges not from expert knowledge or interdisciplinary skills per se, but from the field itself in all its complexity. Indeed, the challenges many communities face are structural and may extend over generations and geographies; they may be both graphically concrete and subtly ideological. With respect to civic discourse, specialized knowledge is but one desired outcome and may be less important for partners than common knowledge and other impacts, such as social recognition, resources, and sensitive policymaking. As cosmographers, students perform as critical design consultants who collaborate with communities and other stakeholders to help effect change in their shared worlds. To help students co-design such worlds, we introduce StudioLab's third critical design frame: *design thinking, a method of human-centered design developed to tackle complex problems found in social and organizational contexts.*

Within our critical design approach, design thinking or DT empowers students to advocate for values of cultural efficacy within systems used to focusing on effectiveness and efficiency, as it explicitly prioritizes human desirability in relation to technical feasibility and financial viability. Moving out into the field, critical design teams can use design thinking to evolve from role-playing to actual consultancy as they engage with communities and other stakeholders. Significantly, design thinking also involves an iterative process of ideation, guided by both *doxa* and *episteme*, and supported by ethnographic research and engineering methods of rapid prototyping

112   J. MCKENZIE

guided by user feedback. Design thinking has been used by both educators and community organizations around the world, and it thus offers StudioLab a robust method of post-Platonic ideation that complements our own production of thought-action figures.

Becoming cosmographer, like becoming maker and becoming builder, can unfold in any field of study, and it may especially attract scholars and students working in public arts and humanities, science communication, public scholarship, participatory research, broader impacts of funded research, translational research, service learning, and university extension programs. Traditionally, research, teaching, and service activities have been separated. StudioLab can help integrate them within the context of community-engaged scholarship in order to address the crisis of the liberal arts. For communities and scholars alike, transmedia knowledge offers a collaborative, design-oriented approach for articulating shared cultural values, advocating within the larger community and developing skills and infrastructures for twenty-first-century civic discourse.

CRITICAL DESIGN 103:
HOW TO DO THINGS WITH WORLDS

This chapter introduces concepts and practices of transmedia knowledge as civic discourse, including models for extending critical design not only across campus but also across communities in the field. In 1955, philosopher J. L. Austin published *How to Do Things with Words*, a book on the power of performative speech acts (e.g., vows and proclamations) to produce actual effects in the world rather than merely describe it.[1] In 2006, conceptual artist Ralo Mayer created *How to Do Things with Worlds*, a collection of texts and images exploring the performative power of models to create the worlds they project.[2] As if to confirm Mayer's insight, in 2008 historian of science Donald MacKenzie published *An Engine, Not a Camera: How Financial Models Shape Markets*.[3] As we will see, researchers of the design thinking process contend that innovation within design

---

[1] J.L. Austen, *How to Do Things With Words* (Cambridge: Harvard University Press, 1962).

[2] Ralo Mayer, *How to Do Things With Worlds 1* (Innsbruck, Austria: Künstlerhaus Büchsenhausen, 2006).

[3] Donald A. MacKenzie, *An Engine Not a Camera: How Financial Models Shape Markets.* (Cambridge, MA: MIT Press, 2006).

teams arises through the active generation of counterfactual statements and the shaping of corresponding alternate worlds—paracosms—with the capacity to become actual. In StudioLab, students use transmedia knowledge to compose cosmograms for integrating different perspectives, discourses, and values. Such cosmograms provide concrete guides for doing things with worlds.

Design Thinking at the d.school

Our first tutor site is the Mecca of contemporary design thinking: Stanford's d.school, whose official name is the Hasso Plattner Institute of Design (dschool.stanford.edu). Its founder, David Kelley, also founded IDEO, a global design firm that extends design thinking's reach around the world. We will describe the d.school's design thinking method in detail below and contextualize it here within the history of design by introducing some relevant cases. We can gauge design thinking's relevance in the title of Peter N. Miller's 2015 *Chronicle of Higher Education* essay, 'Is "Design Thinking" the New Liberal Arts?' Miller cites Harry Elam, Stanford's Vice Provost of Undergraduate Education: 'The d.school is not unlike a center for teaching and learning on steroids: Pedagogy and design thinking inform how to portray content and learning goals.'[4] The d.school's model of design thinking, however, is one of several, even if its embrace across different disciplines and organizations has overshadowed other models. Lucy Kimbell's 'Rethinking Design Thinking' offers a history and typology of design thinking that distinguishes the d.school model as one that approaches design thinking as an *organizational resource*, in contrast to models that approach it as either a *cognitive style of individual designers* or as a *general theory of design*.[5] Kimbell argues that rethinking design thinking involves overcoming the thinking/acting dualism, abandoning the drive for a general definition of design, and displacing the central role of the designer or expert. StudioLab's focus on

---

[4] Peter N. Miller, 'Is Design Thinking the New Liberal Arts?' (The Chronicle of Higher Education, March 26, 2015) Accessed February 15, 2016. https://www.chronicle.com/article/Is-Design-Thinking-the-New/228779.

[5] Lucy Kimbell, 'Rethinking Design Thinking, Part 1' (*Design and Culture*, November 2011), DOI: https://doi.org/10.2752/175470811X13071166525216.

thought-action figures explicitly counters the thinking-acting dualism, and we are drawn to the d.school's model precisely because it does articulate a cognitive style—though one grounded not in individual designers but rather collaborative design teams and their end users. And while it may not be a general theory of design, DT is certainly generalizable or transportable across different domains.

As we will see, the d.school's cognitive style explicitly involves ideation. However, its generation of ideas flows out of *doxa* rather than *episteme*— or rather, *doxa* and *episteme* combine in new ways that lead us to describe this cognitive style as post-Platonic. In modern rhetoric, after the devastation of World War II and the Holocaust, Chaïm Perelman and Lucie Olbrechts-Tyteca helped Hannah Arendt launch the *vita activa* by calling for a 'regressive' philosophy based precisely on the *doxa* of audiences rather than the *episteme* of experts.[6] Within higher education, this grounding in common, rather than expert knowledge, has helped to drive design thinking's use by other colleges and universities As we saw in the Introduction, Smith College's design thinking initiative helps faculty and students with creative problem-solving.[7] Other schools using design thinking include the University of Alabama at Birmingham (student-led creation of a maker space), the University of Maryland at College Park (administrative decision-making), Williams College (curriculum development and research design), and the University of Wisconsin–Madison (engineering courses and research design).[8] Significantly, in July 2018, the Council of Writing Program Administrators (WPA), whose members oversee first-year writing classes nationwide, sponsored a full-day workshop called Design Thinking as WPA Tool: Innovating Curricula, Teaching Practices, and Program Outreach. These initiatives and others indicate that students, faculty, and administrators are already using design thinking to grapple with Plato's Fight Club. For StudioLab, both the d.school's

---

[6] See David Frank and Michelle Bolduc, 'From *vita contemplativa* to *vita activa*: Chaïm Perelman and Lucie Olbrechts-Tyteca's Rhetorical Turn' (*Advances in the History of Rhetoric* Vol. 7), 65–86.

[7] The Design Thinking Initiative. 'The Design Thinking Initiative.' Smith College, Retrieved May 15, 2016. http://smith.edu/design-thinking/

[8] See Lee Gardner, 'How Design Thinking Can Be Applied Across the Campus' (*The Chronicle of Higher Education*, September 10, 2017) www.chronicle.com/article/How-Design-Thinking-Can-Be/241127 and 'Can Design Thinking Redesign Higher Ed?' (*The Chronicle of Higher Education*, September 10, 2017) https://www.chronicle.com/article/Can-Design-Thinking-Redesign/241126.

4 BECOMING COSMOGRAPHER: CO-DESIGNING WORLDS 115

focus on human-centered design and its embrace by different institutions contribute to one of our core missions, to democratize design, while its harmonizing of human desirability, technical feasibility, and financial viability provides a method for another mission, to remix performative values. As we will see, transmedia knowledge as media cascade provides a driving force for the design thinking process.

Community-Based Media at Indigenous Story Studio

A second tutor site is Indigenous Story Studio (ISS), a Canadian organization that collaborates with indigenous communities and public health agencies to produce information comics, videos, and other transmedia knowledge focusing on health, literacy, and wellness issues facing Canadian Aboriginal youth. These issues range from drug addiction and suicide to teenage pregnancy and gang violence. ISS's founder, Sean Muir (Cree, from Peguis First Nation), originally trained in English and film studies before entering the workplace and eventually creating the Healthy Aboriginal Network (HAN) in 2005 to assist indigenous teenagers in British Columbia and across Canada. Weary from reading negative news stories about First Nation families, and realizing that 'no one reads government White Papers,' Muir established HAN as a nonprofit organization and applied for funding from the Vancouver Coastal Health Authority to 'create literacy on health and social issues using comic books.'[9] HAN soon won both provincial and federal funding to produce information comics for youths dealing with suicide prevention, diabetes prevention, maternal child health, and other issues. In 2019, HAN became Indigenous Story Studio (ISS).

From StudioLab's perspective, Indigenous Story Studio is an intimate bureaucracy that has scaled up to a veritable collective assemblage of enunciation: community media-making for Canada's First Nation people. Over the past 15 years, Muir's organization has created over 20 different comics and sold over half a million books, as well as posters and videos. We see here how making media generates the building of collaborative environments, and how both making and building support designing worlds—in this case, a healthier aboriginal world. Muir drew

---

[9] Sean Muir, interview with the author. See "Indigenous Story Studio." Website. Accessed February 22, 2019. https://istorystudio.com/

116   J. MCKENZIE

on his training and business experience to build a network of First Nation authors and illustrators, healthcare and social justice researchers, using funding gleaned from a variety of provincial and federal health organizations. Crucial here is that ISS has not only produced individual works but also *a method and infrastructure for mixing specialized and common knowledge*, bringing together research and everyday situations through a network of people, organizations, and media.

Moreover, ISS's works show the ability of transmedia knowledge to combine Western and indigenous worldviews, often with profound effect. In *Culturally Competent Care: A Case for Culturally Competent Care for Aboriginal Women Giving Birth in Hospital Settings*, researchers Birch, Ruttan, Muth, and Baydala argue that maternal and child healthcare can improve by developing practices better attuned to an aboriginals' own experience of childbirth and health in general.

> In this context, health does not stop at the individual; it includes the relational aspects of life in community. Good or poor health occurs within the experience of family and community health and relationships.... [Whereas] Western health care systems and service providers have traditionally seen the health care provider as the expert and decision maker.[10]

What the authors describe here is a clash of worldviews or ontologies that shape what maternal child care 'is': the West treats childbirth as a trauma or illness, while many aboriginal communities view it as showing health and well-being; hospitals traditionally approach childbirth as a private event, whereas for First Nation peoples it can be a much more social event. Information comics—and transmedia knowledge more generally—offer powerful ways to juxtapose these worlds, stage their differences and commonalities, and empower people to enhance their lives through them.

One of ISS's most popular comics, *It Takes a Village*, addresses aboriginal teenage pregnancy by focusing on basic prenatal care and the role family and community can play in supporting young mothers and their babies.[11] Combining story and argument, author Zoe Hopkins and illus-

---

[10] June Birch, Lia Ruttan, Tracy Muth, and Lola Baydala, 'Culturally Competent Care for Aboriginal Women' (*International Journal of Indigenous Health*, Vol 4, No 2, December 2009): 28, 29.

[11] Zoe Hopkins and Amancay Nahuelpan, Ed. Sean Muir, *It Takes a Village* (n.p: The Healthy Aboriginal Network. 2012).

trator Amancay Hahuelpan create a world composed of common challenges facing pregnant aboriginal teenagers, situating their readers within both realistic and imaginary scenarios. Lively dialogue, supported by shot/reverse shot framing of characters, establishes distinct perspectives that invoke feelings of both distance and empathy, feelings associated, respectively, with expert and common knowledge. Like many information comics, *It Takes a Village* carefully embeds specialized knowledge within narrative exchanges. Lara, the pregnant text-savvy protagonist, ignores her mother's pleas to stay home and rest and instead heads to a party, where she meets Danis, a mysterious young woman with a baby on her back. After Lara considers drinking a beer, for instance, Danis tells her, 'If you drink, you could hurt the way your baby learns and behaves, and she could have physical disabilities, too. For the rest of her life. It's called FASD—fetal alcohol spectrum disorder.'[12] Overcoming Lara's suspicions about her appearance with a child, Danis guides her away from the party and through a series of visions and dreams in which Lara sees her grandmother as a superhero medicine woman, meets her own infant baby playing with its father on a playground, and eventually listens as her mother—represented here as a dog taking care of puppies and a fawn—tells her that babies must be held in order to bond and feel love. In these revelatory scenes, the differences between modern and traditional cultures play out within Lara herself, as she, and the readers who empathize with her, learn that each world offers valuable knowledge and resources. The entire narrative world folds back on itself as Lara learns that Danis is her own daughter and the baby on her back her own granddaughter, thus positioning Lara herself as a superwoman grandmother.

Transmedia knowledge and collaborative creativity can create small worlds where different knowledges and different ontologies co-exist, similar to the liminal and liminoid spaces Victor Turner described, where cultural symbols may be questioned and rearranged.[13] In this light, Lara's vision of her grandmother, a gray-haired woman wearing a red bathrobe and blue Superman shirt, can be seen here to become a cosmographic thought-action figure: 'Super Gran.' Lara's Super Gran gathers together elements from the four quadrants of Ulmer's cosmogram: family (grandmother), community (First Nation), discipline (public health), and pop

---

[12] Ibid.
[13] Victor Turner, 'Liminal to Liminoid, in Play, Flow, and Ritual: An Essay in Comparative Symbology' (Rice Institute Pamphlet–Rice University Studies, 60, no. 3m 1974).

culture (Superman). Here we find one lesson of *It Takes a Village*. 'Lara: "What—that my Gran's a little old superhero?" Danis: "Exactly. She has so much knowledge and power. You could learn so much from her."' Incarnated in a First Nation superwoman, this lesson of knowledge and power, of course, resonates with the comic's broader lesson: precisely, *it takes a village to care for a mother and child*. Significantly, it also took a village to make *It Takes a Village*. As it often does, the Indigenous Story Studio designed community input into its production process, sharing with community youths a motion comic draft, a narrated video made with storyboard drawings, to get feedback and fine-tune the work in process. Muir says that community feedback has really improved the impact of ISS's comics. For StudioLab, Super Gran thus figures a wide collaborative creativity, that of the First Nations people. As we will see, human-centered design thinking begins its process with fieldwork and feedback.

Participatory Research with the Ella Baker Center for Human Rights

The next tutor site demonstrates the central role that transmedia knowledge and collaborative design can play in community-based participatory research, research where *episteme* and *doxa* mix for strategic purposes. In 2015, the Ella Baker Center for Human Rights in Los Angeles, California, in collaboration with Forward Together, Research Action Design, and over 20 other US community organizations, launched the research project *Who Pays? The True Cost of Incarceration on Families* ellabaker-center.org/who-pays-the-true-cost-of-incarceration-on-families. Focused on the direct and indirect costs of incarceration on individuals, families, and communities, this participatory research project unfolded across 14 states and consisted of interviews and surveys with 712 formerly incarcerated people, 368 family members, and 27 employers, as well as 34 focus groups with family members and individuals.[14] While incarceration is a widely recognized and researched topic, the *Who Pays?* project brings a Research Justice approach that privileges engaging the many people affected by the criminal justice system. 'Grounded in a transformative research agenda, this research also seeks to center community knowledge and leadership in movements for social change.'[15] Coordinated by trained

---

[14] Saneta deVuono-powell, et al, *Who Pays? The True Cost of Incarceration on Families* (Oakland, CA: Ella Baker Center, Forward Together, Research Action Design, 2015): 7.
[15] Saneta deVuono-powell, et al., *Who Pays?*, 51.

4 BECOMING COSMOGRAPHER: CO-DESIGNING WORLDS   119

researchers through the different community organizations, *Who Pays?* is research conducted on communities, by communities, and for communities. The informants of social science fieldwork here can become the local researchers' own community members of family, friends, neighbors, and co-workers.

Significantly, the project's research sought to 'address the lack of representation and the misrepresentation of low-income communities of color in the design of smart solutions that can break the cycles of violence and poverty exacerbated by the criminal justice system at the local, state, and national levels.'[16] In short, *Who Pays?* situates itself in relation to a larger design project, the design of smart solutions—not a universal blueprint implemented from above but responsive solutions that emerge through local actors, thus, depending on the situation, enabling different forms to take shape. Traditionally, disciplinary expertise—whether it be in social policy, philosophy, or design—orients itself by establishing its superiority over other knowledges, often misrepresenting them: *episteme* over *doxa*. Justice Research and other participatory research approaches seek not to overthrow expertise but transform its function by bringing common knowledge, *doxa*, on to the stage and, giving it a leading role. Thus, the research of *Who Pays?* reflects the experiences of families across the US and seeks community alternatives to existing social policies. Here we see how Justice Research and human-centered design intersect in the design of smart solutions: both remix *episteme* and *doxa* and displace expert knowledge with a more general knowledge.

The research design of *Who Pays?* also outlined the publication and dissemination of research findings and recommendations to different stakeholders, including community members, policymakers, other researchers, and the general public. Here we find exemplary uses of transmedia knowledge as civic discourse. At the center is a 60-page report on the ways that incarceration affects individuals and their families and communities. Tellingly, the report takes the form not of a standard white paper (single-sided 8.5 × 11-inch paper, double-spaced 12-point font, with few, if any, images), but instead a sharply designed, full-color report with photographs, diagrams, infographics, and text printed double-sided, thus creating two-page spreads like those found in magazines. The report is available in PDF format for free download. In addition, the Ella Baker website features photographs of a community event that functioned as a research installa-

---

[16] Ibid., 50.

tion and launch party, showing how large prints of graphs and quotes from the report cover the walls and community members stand before them discussing the research while others listen to speakers as they consume food and drink. For StudioLab, this social form of research symposium (from the Greek *sun* 'together' + *potēs* 'drinker') offers the simplest and most direct way of enmeshing epistemic knowledge within common knowledge, for unfolding argument and evidence alongside intimate stories and reflections with a collaboratively designed alternative world. Together, the *Who Pays?* report, website, and community events demonstrate the power of transmedia knowledge to function as civic discourse across a wide range of audiences and stakeholders. When teamed with participatory research, transmedia knowledge can become self-generative and transformative in sustainable, scalable ways.

Digital Engagements at Imagining America

Our final tutor site is *Public*, the blog of Imagining America (IA), a national organization of scholars, artists, designers, humanists, and community organizers dedicated to 'public scholarship, cultural organizing, and campus change that inspires collective imagination, knowledge-making, and civic action on pressing public issues. By dreaming and building together in public, IA creates the conditions to shift culture and transform inequitable institutional and societal structures.'[17] 'Building and dreaming together' captures the process of becoming cosmographer or co-designer of possible worlds, while cultural organizing refers to the use of art-making and other cultural activities as forms of social organizing and community engagement. StudioLab connects practices of cultural organizing to analogous practices developed for community engagement in the sciences, social sciences, and professions.

The IA blog functions as an online journal with articles, reviews, and case studies composed of text, images, and videos. Significantly, *Public* Volume 4, Issue 2 explores 'Digital Engagements; Or, the Virtual Gets Real' and directly addresses the challenges and opportunities of scholars engaging communities through cultural organizing featuring digital

---

[17] Imagining America, Mission statement (https://imaginingamerica.org/about/). Accessed January 28, 2019.

media.[18] 'Digital Engagements' thus constitutes a tutor site packed with tutor cases dealing with issues of racism, climate change, HIV stigmatization, and basic questions of representation and civic participation through the use of media forms ranging from oral narratives to visual and social media to alternative reality games and online courses. Cultural organizing refers to such uses of art and other cultural activities as forms activism and social engagement. Several crucial insights run through 'Digital Engagements.' First, the products of cultural organizing—videos, images, stories—are usually as important as the process of their production—the actual making and sharing of media. Second, the value of both products and process depends on the underlying relationship between campus and community collaborators. Creating, building, and maintaining the community relationship takes precedence over any particular engagement project. The relationship forms the basic platform of community engagement and is often shaped by sharp economic, technological, cultural, and educational differences between campus and community partners. Finally, digital media and cultural organizing have the potential to build and enhance these relationships—and to weaken and destroy them. In short, 'Digital Engagements: The Virtual Gets Real' reveals the pharmakological dimension of transmedia knowledge as civic discourse.

In the *Public* article 'The Art of Transformation: Cultural Organizing by Reinventing Media,' collaborators from the University of Maryland–Baltimore County (UMBC) and Baltimore community organizations report on a multi-year project exploring which 'media—as tools for collective thinking—has the capacity we need to create positive social change?'[19] At the core of the Art of Transformation (AoT) project is the MapTu software platform for gathering, deliberating, and sharing diverse knowledges in a virtual 3D environment that combines archiving of community media, geomapping of resources, data visualization, and predictive modeling (See Fig. 4.1). Long term, the project seeks to enable community members to engage in collaborative data analytics and thus better inform decision-making and policy formation.

---

[18] See Teresa Mangum, 'Welcome to Digital Engagements; Or, the Virtual Gets Real' (*Public* 4 (2) http://public.imaginingamerica.org/blog/issues/digital-engagements-when-the-virtual-gets-real/).

[19] Frank Anderson, et al. 'The Art of Transformation: Cultural Organizing by Reinventing Media.' (*Public* 4:2 http://public.imaginingamerica.org/blog/article/the-art-of-transformation-cultural-organizing-by-reinventing-media/ Accessed 2/10/2019).

122   J. MCKENZIE

Cities are rapidly moving toward data analytics to see their challenges more clearly, to draw connections between disparate data, and to engineer solutions. If such solutions fail to take into account the human stories and sociocultural factors made tangible through the arts, and if everyday residents of the city are not involved in cocreating such knowledge, efforts will fail.[20]

Here we find a compelling vision for the ways transmedia knowledge can function as civic discourse, enabling local communities to represent themselves and participate in wider discussions, deliberations, and decision-making. The proposed vision of a virtual public square offers something akin to Google Earth meets community centers, meets Greek agora. However, vision is one thing, delivery another, and in between lies the design process.

The AoT project resonates with StudioLab's third mission, to mix performative values. By combining cultural organizing with collaborative analytics, AoT hopes to bridge the gap between qualitative stories and images, on the one hand, and quantitative information and data, on the other. In our terms, AoT seeks to inject values of cultural efficacy into data-driven decision-making where values of effectiveness and efficiency predominate. Under development at UMBC, the MapTu platform's research design includes community input generated by the AoT team of researchers and community organizations. However, as its *Public* article frankly admits, the AoT's initial digital engagement efforts, videotaping and sharing back interviews of local residents, wound up threatening the underlying community relationship rather than building on it. The collaborators write: 'Those living in communities ignored or maligned by media feel the impact of the perceptions media has created. People's strongest critiques were about representation in our editing room and in communities. [...] Community members did not make the media.'[21] In short, AoT's collaborative platform did not reach out far enough to connect campus and community. The AoT's article offers a frank evaluation of its own missteps and articulates ways to include the community in making media by creating or finding spaces and practices for doing so. They acknowledge that the 'the software and cultural organizing practices must attend to creating sacred, safe, and brave spaces, clarifying values and principles, and developing practices to support multiple perspectives and deliberation.'[22]

---

[20] Frank Anderson, et al, 'The Art of Transformation: Cultural Organizing by Reinventing Media.'
[21] Ibid.
[22] Ibid.

For StudioLab, the Art of Transformation and Imagining America's other cases of digital engagement illustrate ways that scholars and communities are already collaborating through media and by cultural organizing. Digital engagement is not a panacea but brings both promise and risk, as does any community engagement initiative. The creation and sharing of individual media forms are themselves connected to underlying material issues of representation and resources, form and content, knowledge and power. To connect the experiences of campus and community partners, we approach each as desiring-machines with shared experiences and collaborative platforms of discourses and practices. As AoT suggests, community members may themselves become makers of media and builders of platforms—or already be makers and builders. Collaborative shared experiences form the building blocks of productive community relationships, as they build experiential architectures connecting campus and communities.

Community Engagement and Transmedia Knowledge

The emergence of transmedia knowledge comes at a propitious time, as higher education seeks to renew its relations with local communities and society at large. As the tutor sites demonstrate, transmedia knowledge and human-centered design can connect seminar, studio, and lab spaces—the spaces of epistemic knowledge—with a fourth space, the doxic field of community engagement. In countries around the world, recent political and economic crises have sharpened stark divisions between urban and rural populations, between those with college degrees and those without, between those with digital access and those lacking it, and between social groups vying for recognition and justice in the name of different nations, religions, ethnicities, races, genders, sexualities, abilities, ages, and other identities. While campuses worldwide seek to engage new realities off-campus, they also grapple on-campus with debates and protests on issues ranging from free speech, immigration, labor, discrimination, access, sexual harassment, diversity, education funding, the corporatization of research, and curriculum design. As divided as the epistemic fields and disciplines may be, they share *logos* and *eidos* and the medium of alphabetic writing, and thus all argue and debate in scholarly journals. Connecting the ideas and logic of *episteme* with the images and stories of *doxa*, transmedia knowledge and human-centered design offer ways to help transform the academy inside and out.

124   J. MCKENZIE

StudioLab has developed workshops, courses, and assignments designed to help instructors and students use transmedia knowledge to extend or enhance research and learning in the public field. In most cases, faculty and institutions have standing relationships with community partners and seek to explore ways that transmedia knowledge can serve community needs and strengthen collaboration. At national workshops conducted for the NARRTC (formerly the National Association of Rehabilitation Research and Training Centers) and for the Cornell Translational Research Summer Institute, participants were encouraged to approach transmedia knowledge as a way to reframe the broader impact of their work by envisioning new audiences and/or affordances for it. As we have seen, the forms, functions, and audiences of transmedia knowledge vary widely: info comics, PechaKuchas, posters, videos, and so on can serve as a means of self-representation and storytelling, translating knowledge, advocating policy, and conducting research while targeting a diverse set of stakeholders, including community members, policymakers, and the general public.

We have already described how transformational the building of collaborative platforms can be for those making transmedia knowledge and sharing experiences, ideas, and media while role-playing as critical design teams. Co-designing worlds can have a similar effect on knowledge itself. Our analogy for this transformation: transmediating knowledge for the field is like placing it in a magic lantern that projects outward new audiences, new perspectives, and new uses for this same knowledge. A 2017 transmedia workshop conducted at Siena College, a small liberal arts school near Albany, NY, demonstrates this generative potential. Hosted by Ruth Kassel, Assistant Director Academic Community Engagement at Siena, this StudioLab workshop teamed up faculty, students, and members of the Underground Railroad History Project (URHP) to explore ways to support the Stephen and Harriet Myers Residence, a home that had once been part of the nineteenth-century Underground Railroad activity. The Myers were an African American abolitionist couple, and the URHP is committed to sharing their story and the relevance of black abolitionists today. Restoring the Myers' home as a historic site entails connecting its forgotten history to different sets of stakeholders, including historians, contemporary neighbors, potential donors, and the wider general public.

In our workshop, teams first learned different transmedia forms along with the CAT and UX design frames; they then selected different historical artifacts—public flyers about the Underground Railroad, photographs of key local figures, and bottles of hair tonic found on the site—and used the frames to explore resonances between these artifacts and different stakeholders, around which they sketched transmedia campaigns designed to appeal to each group. Teams later presented their campaign ideas to one another, with one team proposing posters for local beauty salons that would publicize the Stephen and Harriet Myers Residence by featuring the beauty products unearthed on the site, thus connecting past and present neighborhood residents through shared experiences of personal care.

Here we find imaginative problem-solving far from discipline, unfolding in the field of community engagement as historical artifacts become reanimated as they pass through different media genres for a range of different possible audiences. Transmedia knowledge's magic lantern effects—its array of media forms and design frames operating like a planetarium projector—can help researchers and community partners alike identify different constellations of Whys, Whats, and Hows for engaging different audiences, each constellation composed of specific calls to adventure and calls to action in the world. Through transmedia, the transformational potential of specialized and common knowledge emerges in the lives of students and community members. In the field, *episteme* experiences a renaissance in the *doxa* of everyday life.

CRITICAL DESIGN TEAMS IN THE FIELD

On campus, StudioLab's critical design teams move students transversally through activities traditionally siloed far away from one other. Working as teams, students perform conceptual activities associated with seminar spaces common in the humanities and social sciences; working as bands, teams hone aesthetic skills found in studio spaces of art and design departments; and working in guilds, students focus on technical skills found in the lab spaces of science and engineering. Moving out into the field, critical design teams take on the role of consultants, sharing their conceptual, aesthetic, and technical skills as well as their intimate bureaucratic or organizational sensibilities within the context of community engagement and co-designing worlds.

As consultants in the field, critical design teams can draw on practices of critical performativity described by Critical Management Studies scholars. Recall that the power circuits of efficiency-effectiveness that define Lyotardian performativity govern not just the production of contemporary knowledge but also social bonds, and this governance takes the form of performance-driven outcomes and assessment in institutions ranging from universities and businesses to community and nonprofit organizations. Critical performativity seeks to supplement the pervasive drive for efficiency-effectiveness with resignifying practices associated with Butlerian performativity, practices that include refunctioning both discursive and nondiscursive forms. It is here that values of cultural efficacy—of doing the right thing for people—can enter into processes of discussion, evaluation, and decision-making. In the case of Indigenous Story Studio, this means framing important health, financial, and social information in characters and narratives reflective of the culture of indigenous communities; in the case of *What Cost? The True Cost of Incarceration on Families*, it means countering the stereotypes associated with affected community members with accurate representation of their lives and values and ensuring that these inform relevant social policy; in the case of the Art of Transformation, it means ensuring that campus and community members build shared experiences and collaborative platforms that empower people to improve their everyday lives through cultural organizing and collaborative analytics.

Critical design teams can foreground the importance of different performative values in both their own project work and the lives of community members. The micro-emancipations of critical performativity involve a transvaluation of performative values that introduces or enhances values of cultural efficacy, while revalorizing those of organizational efficiency and technical effectiveness. Without attention to efficacy, collaborations quickly become misguided as they fail to serve participants' underlying needs and aspirations; without attention to effectiveness and efficiency, collaborations tend to lack consistency, scalability, and sustainability. The goal for consultants is thus to encourage and support the remix or retuning of performative values.

Not surprisingly, transmedia knowledge can play a crucial role here, as revealed in a workshop conducted with the Patient Care Advocacy Team (PCAT), a volunteer program in Ithaca, New York, run by the Cayuga Medical Center, Cornell Public Service Center, and Ithaca College's Center for Civic Engagement. PCAT connects students with patient care teams in the medical center's in-patient and emergency departments, where they support patient comfort and advocacy. As part of their community engagement, students reflect on their experience in a written text and digital story, and our workshop focused on shaping stories through posters, comics, and PechaKuchas that would be shared with hospital administrators. In the course of the workshop, we learned that the medical center had noted an improvement in patient care as measured by their patient surveys. This information helped students reframe the transmedia project before them: their reflective stories could become part of a larger story, the success of patient-centered practices in a large, community hospital as told by its own measures of performance assessment. Transmedia knowledge that arises from concrete, lived experiences can provide salient qualitative evidence (and thus a potential measure) of cultural efficacy, and thereby help students and community partners better articulate their own needs and desires within formal assessment and decision-making processes. This qualitative dimension pervades data analysis: to be comprehensible and persuasive, data must be visualized, those visualizations wrapped in arguments and stories, and those arguments and stories shared with appropriate stakeholders. Critical design teams and their partners can use transmedia knowledge to visualize data, tell stories, make arguments, and advocate for particular goals with a wide variety of audiences. In such ways, transmedia knowledge becomes civic discourse.

DESIGN FRAME 3: DESIGN THINKING

StudioLab's final design frame, design thinking or DT, also provides the third element of our critical design pedagogy, alongside critical thinking's tradition of argumentative writing and tactical media's subversive activism. Design thinking offers a comprehensive design process that directly addresses StudioLab's mission to inject values of cultural efficacy into systems dominated by technical effectiveness and organizational efficiency. Tim Brown, the CEO of IDEO, defines design thinking as balancing three related constraints: technical feasibility, financial viability, and human desirability.

> Constraints can best be visualized in terms of three overlapping criteria for successful ideas: feasibility (what is functionally possible within the foreseeable future); viability (what is likely to become part of a sustainable business model); and desirability (what makes sense to people and for people). A competent designer will resolve each of these constraints, but a *design thinker* will bring them into a harmonious balance.[23]

---

[23] Tim Brown, *Change by Design* (New York: HarperCollins, 2009), 18.

128   J. MCKENZIE

Desirability, feasibility, and viability closely align with the performative values of cultural efficacy, technical effectiveness, and organizational efficiency. As a method of human-centered design applied to organizational and social problems, design thinking begins with human desirability, and for this reason, it offers StudioLab a powerful, ready-made approach for helping teams and their partners use transmedia knowledge to balance highly quantitative measures of effectiveness and efficiency with more qualitative assessments of efficacy.

Like many design methods, DT takes an iterative approach which encourages participants to 'fail fast' in order to succeed faster, repeating steps and altering designs by adjusting to feedback at any stage along the way. Projects may last days, weeks, months, or years; so iterative loops can be short or long. Keeping this iterability in mind, design thinking's process, which critical design teams practice first in class and then in the field, unfolds across five phases: *empathize, define, ideate, prototype*, and *test*.

1. *Empathize.* Throughout its process, design thinking uses a transdisciplinary approach, employing different methods at different moments, beginning first by empathizing with others using fieldwork methods drawn from ethnography and sociology. Human-centered design begins with humans, with learning about their needs and desires concerning a particular problem at a deep level. Through interviews and observations, design teams learn people's behaviors as well as their cognitive understanding of the situation. The teams then dig down to elicit the underlying feelings, beliefs, and values of those involved. According to Brown, in order to gain empathy with people 'we need to begin by recognizing that their seemingly inexplicable behaviors represent different strategies for coping with the confusing, complex, and contradictory world they live in.'[24] The goal of this phase is to get into the shoes of people, overcome one's own preconceptions about the situation, and understand it from their perspective at a deep, systemic level.

One way StudioLab trains students in design thinking uses a customized version of the d.school exercise redesigning the backpack which teaches the DT process to novice designers in 60–90 minutes. Created by Dee Warmath at the University of Wisconsin–Madison, the Redesigning the Process of Carrying Stuff workshop enhances a widely used exercise developed by the d.school, reframing the problem and opens the design

---

[24] Tim Brown, *Change by Design*, 49.

challenge beyond backpacks.[25] Working in pairs, one student role-plays as designer, interviewing their partner and writing down: how they carry their personal belongings, the ways they feel about doing so, and any issues they have with the process. After taking a moment to review their notes, interviewers dig deeper, asking follow-up questions that probe into the underlying feelings and values at stake for their partners, again recording their responses in writing. The students then reverse roles and repeat this first phase, with the interviewer becoming the interviewee and vice versa.

In practice out in the field, design teams may spend hours, days, or weeks in the empathize phase, observing and interviewing community partners and collecting stories and images. At the end of this phase, teams should gather and unpack all their research with a single visualization, using such 'shared media' as notes, photos, Post-its, and diagrams to spatialize what they have learned. In StudioLab terms: critical design teams transmediate the situation into small comprehensive installations that spatialize ideas through artifacts and thus translate the field into studio space. In design thinking terms, such shared media is crucial to the overall design process, helping to record, nourish, and generate design solutions. As we will see, shared media is transmedia knowledge that takes different forms and serves different functions in the design thinking process. Here the spatialization of research both documents the first phase research and helps transition to the second phase.

2. *Define.* Design thinking's second 'define' phase synthesizes the insights generated through the empathy phase and seeks to describe the underlying situation in a clear and concise definition or problem statement. Defining is sense-making, clearly articulating the design challenge at hand. Teams make sense of the field research spatialized in the installation of artifacts by using them to focus the design challenge as narrowly as possible. All the research, all the artifacts now become transmediated into a single statement that describes the partner and their needs and articulates the problem space, an open space that emerges from insights about the design challenge.

In the Redesigning the Process of Carrying Stuff exercise, the students' observations and discussions from the first phase often begin to reveal basic desires and underlying values that had not yet been fully articulated, and that only begin to crystalize after phase one. Patterns emerge: 'fashionable' and 'attractive'; 'well-made,' 'long-lasting,' and 'high-quality';

---

[25] Dee Warmath, "Redesigning the Process of Carrying Stuff." Unpublished worksheet.

'lots of stuff,' 'baggy,' and 'over-sized'; and 'back pain' and 'posture'. In the define phase, students synthesize their insights—for example, beneath aesthetic and economic needs lie functional and health needs—into a clear problem statement, one that opens up an imaginative space that frames and limits the problem and gives specific criteria to drive creativity. *To carry her stuff, Charlie needs something large and durable that looks good and takes care of her back.* Note that this problem statement leaves 'what's needed' undefined while providing discrete attributes that synthesize many desires and values into a nexus of potential solutions. 'It may seem counterintuitive but crafting a more narrowly focused problem statement tends to yield both greater quantity and higher quality solutions when you are generating ideas.'[26]

In practice, the shift between the first two design phases reveals the shift between *divergent and convergent thinking*, a rhythm important to design thinking. In the empathize phase, design teams generate many observations and stories and may go off in many directions, while in the define phase, teams narrow their thinking and converge toward a single point of view. This rhythm between divergence and convergence resonates with the flow and break, as well as the dispersion and return, of thought and action. Problem statements are actionable statements: produced by convergent thinking, they trigger divergent thinking in the third phase of critical design thinking. Narrowing produces a sudden opening of unforeseen possibilities: the written statement now becomes transmediated into multiple forms.

3. *Ideate.* Design thinking is creative, and its signature creation occurs in its third phase, ideation. Using the potentiality of the design space its constraints, and the criteria of the problem statement, teams generate ideas by any means necessary: brainstorming, bodystorming, chance operations, displacements, reframings, and so on. Divergent thinking takes over, everyone suspends judgment and makes up as many different solutions as possible. Problems may be divided up, their parts rearranged and solved in various ways, and solutions then recombined in surreal form. The goal is to generate not four or five ideas but scores, even hundreds of ideas, whether written, drawn, or otherwise configured. Teams move

---

[26] 'An Introduction to Design Thinking: Process Guide,' n.p. Hasso Plattner Institute of Design, Stanford University. Accessed January 12, 2019 https://dschool-old.stanford.edu/sandbox/groups/designresources/wiki/36873/attachments/74b3d/ModeGuideBOOTCAMP2010L.pdf

beyond initial, obvious solutions to truly unexpected and novel figures of thought-action. This creativity is collective and shared rather than individual and private. It is infectious rather than neurotic.

When teaching students design thinking's ideation phase, by using Redesigning the Process of Carrying Stuff, we call attention to how Warmath's enhanced workshop redefines and reframes the original d.school's exercise: the design challenge shifts from redesigning an object to reconfiguring an entire activity. In StudioLab workshops, students have generated ideas for extraordinary backpacks—but also a wide array of other ways to carry stuff. When performing this exercise, students ideate on their own; in the field, they collaborate, and the number and variety of ideas dramatically increase.

Although this phase of design thinking is called 'ideation,' for StudioLab these ideas are at post-Platonic: they emerge from *doxa*, not as *episteme* opposed to it but as a regressive mix of common and expert knowledge. Further, they emerge as much from abductive leaps and conductive flashes as from inductive and deductive steps. The goal is not The Idea but ideas, and lots of them. Within teams, these para-eidetic forms emerge collectively rather than from an individual thinker or psyche. Indeed, they are less ideas than thought-action figures. Ideas are frozen, static; figures are shimmering, dynamic. Ideas, figures, and thought-actions—all emerge from, as, and into shared media, different forms of transmedia knowledge unfolding here in a design process whose end is not ideation but something else: the production of prototypes. Transitioning into the next design phase, convergent thinking returns as teams focus in and select three distinct ideas to make into working artifacts using criteria from the design challenge, emergent frameworks, or even stock categories, such as 'most sensible,' 'most extreme,' and 'most surprising' to guide the design of functional prototypes.

4. *Prototype.* The d.school defines prototyping as the 'iterative generation of artifacts.'[27] In the prototyping phase, designers' narrowing of attention into the making of things—drawings, models, objects, storyboards, role-playing scenarios—transmediates ideas into actual stuff in the world. Prototypes are low res, low cost ways to try out different ideas with partners, fail fast, and iterate. Form follows failure. Sharing a series of prototypes with partners allows teams to explore and develop the experience design of emerging ideas and processes. Rough prototypes become

---

[27] 'An Introduction to Design Thinking' n.p.

132   J. MCKENZIE

successively refined, evolving from low res, abstract renderings to high res, concrete forms through the iterative feedback of human-centered design. Thinking emerges from making media and building experiences.

In its DT training exercise's prototyping phase, StudioLab offers students an array of arts and crafts materials for generating artifacts, including construction paper, string, buttons, paper clips, markers, glue, Play-Doh, pipe cleaners, and plastic figures. Given a time constraint of about 15–20 minutes, each student mock-ups a single prototype, often a small-scale model of some creative way for their partners to carry their stuff—from backpacks to pouches, purses, briefcases, belts, lockers, and wagons—all carefully designed and crafted by hand. Students often comment on the transformative force of this prototyping phase, for they both witness and carry out the incarnation of ideas and desires in material form.

In the field, the design process further narrows, as thinking continues to converge. Prototyping helps clarify and refine the problem statement, the challenge driving the entire process, and comparison between different prototypes enables further distinctions and choices. While at any time an idea may be scratched and the design process restarted, the process typically narrows efforts around selecting and developing one idea for testing in the final phase. The selection criteria are always context specific and emergent, although values of human desirability inform the prototyping, whose processes themselves demonstrate levels of technical feasibility, and perhaps even financial viability. Indeed, over the arc of the design process, the performative values themselves evolve through effectiveness and efficiency, guided by the primacy of efficacy.

5. *Test.* In the fifth phase, design teams solicit formal feedback about their prototypes, again working closely with partners to observe and discuss their interactions. The goal is to once again dig deeper, but while the empathy phase was broad and divergent, testing further narrows and focuses the convergent thinking of the prototyping phase. Testing slightly different versions of the prototype, whether these be objects or experiences, generates more and more refined understandings of the design challenge. If possible, testing should occur in real-life context or scenarios that match them closely. Role-playing can also be used. Teams test their solutions and also their basic understanding of the problem.

With redesigning the process of carrying your stuff, students present their rough prototypes to their partners in the testing phase. As with formal testing, the general rule is to show rather than tell: set the design before the partner and let them interact with it on their own. Their explorations, comments, and questions provide crucial feedback and direction for designers, who should seek answers about specific aspects of their design while also being open to new and expected insights. What designers test here, is the experience design as much as the actual object or process—or rather, the entwining of experience and artifact reveals how well human desirability incarnates itself within the limits of the prototype's technical feasibility.

This DT exercise's short time-frame precludes research into the design's financial viability, but out in the field, solving problems entails addressing issues of scalability and sustainability—and the value of efficiency. Rapid prototyping facilities enable designers to test a series of increasingly high-resolution designs, narrowing and refining the nexus of desirability, feasibility, and viability through iterations of trial and error. Indeed, the entire design thinking process may repeat several times before details of manufacturing and delivery come to the fore. The iterative process, however, ensures that human desirability informs even the final phases of design. The resulting design is thus not so much an isolated artifact or stand-alone process but rather a thing or process arising out of a larger, ongoing situation—a small life-world or tiny cosmos. Through the design thinking process, this world emerges.

Co-consulting and Transmedia Cultural Organizing

How one uses the design thinking frame in the field will depend on the community relationship and academic context in question. The following approach is based on two community-engaged courses at Cornell University with graduate students and upper-class students collaborating with teenagers in different after-school programs run by two community partners, the Ithaca Urban 4H Program and the George Junior Republic School (GJR) in Freeville, New York. Unique among Ivy League schools, Cornell is half private and half public, as it is also a land-grant research university. The Cornell Cooperative Extension oversees 4H organizations throughout New York, including the Ithaca Urban 4H Program. GJR and Urban 4H and their members have different backgrounds and needs, and Cornell's Public Service Center maintains long-term relationships with them and other community partners. Both after-school programs have ongoing media projects: at GJR, teens involved in the juvenile court system participate in two Poetic Justice poetry clubs focusing on issues of identity, expression, and literacy; while at Urban 4H, teens from the Karen immigrant community are creating a mural depicting their harrowing trek from Myanmar to Thailand to America. Through the Public Service Center, the two programs reached out, and ongoing collaborations emerged over two semesters: one focused on transmediating the GJR teens' poems into digital media, the other on 4H teens creating comics based on personal experience of the trek or any other interest. The courses were designed to mesh with these existing shared experiences and collaborative platforms (Fig. 4.2).

In class, StudioLab's approach begins by preparing students for cultural organizing by first learning about the partners' communities and their specific projects: the project goals, their processes, and the partner's underlying missions. Between student and community member, there may be campus offices, community organizations, and liaisons, each layer having its own story and evaluative framework that informs the collaboration. As much as possible, we take these frames into account, for each function as a

Fig. 4.2 Cornell students Rachel Whalen and Catherine Giese consult with George Junior Republic students on transmediating their poetry. (Photo by author)

transmediation of knowledge. Students then begin learning StudioLab's three design frames, including the Redesign the Process of Carrying Stuff workshop and its focus on listening and empathy. Students first learn the frames' components conceptually, see them immediately demonstrated with examples, and then learn them 'by hand' through exercises, before taking the learning process out into the field. In a class engaged with both community partners, students role-played as a community-based design firm composed of two teams, one working with GJR and the other Urban 4H. By learning the background stories of their partners, studying and practicing the design frames, and role-playing as critical design teams, students become media makers and platform builders before attempting to become cosmographers.

To fine-tune the learning experiences and transformative potential in the field for both students and community members, StudioLab has developed a co-consultancy process, in which students and community members alternate and role-play as design consultants for one another. Alongside the partners' projects, students develop a transmedia project connecting their own studies with teenage audiences, which they present to partners for feedback. In this way, both students and partners play expert and novice, designer and consultant. Overall, the co-consultancy process takes everyone outside themselves, not just physically through an exchange of visits, but also experientially as they role-play in real collaboration with others. This is precisely the power of shared experiences and collaborative platforms: to generate experiential architectures that connect and transform people through transmedia knowledge and cultural organizing. At the same time, the co-consultancy process ensures that students and community partners clarify their interests and pursue them in ways beneficial to the underlying relationship.

HCD and Performative Transvaluation

Design thinking provides a robust method for critical design teams to address StudioLab's third mission: the transvaluation or remixing of values of culturally efficacious performance, technologically effectiveness performance, and organizationally efficient performance—what we can call the 3Ps of Mission 3. In describing desirability, feasibility, and viability as constraints, Brown also situates them in relation to three spaces of innovation:

The continuum of innovation is best thought of as a system of overlapping spaces rather than a sequence of orderly steps. We can think of them as *inspiration*, the problem or opportunity that motivates the search for solutions; *ideation*, the process of generating, developing, and testing ideas; and *implementation*, the path that leads from the project room to the market. Projects may loopback thought these spaces more than once as the teams refines its ideas and explores new directions.[28]

These three spaces can help us clarify the design thinking process and the roles played by different forms of shared, transmedia knowledge used by teams working collaboratively in the field.

The design thinking process has been simplified in the context of international aid and development. IDEO, working with the Bill and Melinda Gates Foundation, International Development Enterprise, Heifer International, and the International Center for Research on Women, developed the *Human-Centered Design Toolkit* to document and support uses of design thinking for people living under $2 per day. Here financial viability forcibly informs human desirability and technical feasibility. Significantly, this toolkit offers a leaner version of the design thinking process, articulating it in just three phases: Hear, Create, and Deliver, which the toolkit's authors and graphic designers map into the same initials—HCD—as those of Human-Centered Design. Hear, Create, and Deliver also maps on to the three spaces of innovation and the three constraints of desirability, feasibility, and viability.[29] These mappings and configurations concretize the role of design thinking in StudioLab's critical design approach and its third mission of performative transvaluation.

The toolkit's Hear phase corresponds to Brown's spaces of inspiration and human desirability, and it includes the process of empathizing—listening to community members and learning their perspectives, feelings, and values. The Create phase synthesizes field research into a defining problem statement and then uses it to generate and select from new concrete possibilities. It corresponds to the spaces of ideation and technical feasibility and includes the processes of defining, ideating, and initial prototyping. The Deliver phase further refines and concretizes ideas, testing them with partners in real-life situations, and then making final adjustments before deploying them in the

---

[28] Tim Brown, *Change by Design*, 16.

[29] IDEO. *Human-Centered Design Toolkit*. 2009. https://www.ideo.com/work/human-centered-design-toolkit/. 6–9.

field. It corresponds to the spaces of implementation and financial viability, and it includes the processes of prototyping and testing. (Hear, Create, and Deliver, we will note, also resonates strongly with Duarte's three-part narrative sparkline and LeFever's Why, What, and How, and thereby reveals the experience design of design thinking itself.)

HCD provides critical design teams with a three-letter thought-action figure for overlaying design thinking with StudioLab's mission of remixing the 3Ps of efficacy, effectiveness, and efficiency. The Hear, Create, Deliver of human-centered design orchestrates a space-time of different performances: *hearing* community members brings efficacious performance to the fore and guides the *creation* of effective performances and the *delivery* of efficient performances, which each in their turn also come to the fore. For community partners, this focus on performative values, sharpened and shared by transmedia knowledge and deployed in different social and organizational contexts, can help community members better represent their experiences, advocate for rights and resources, and inform decision- and policymaking. In taking up Mission 3, it is here that critical design teams can best assist partners with transmedia knowledge and performative transvaluation.

Shared Media and the Orchestration of Performances

HCD and the orchestration of efficacious, effective, and efficient performances can also help us clarify further the roles played by different forms of shared, transmedia knowledge in the design thinking process. Design thinking has generated its own body of formal research: design thinking research studies such topics as collaboration, creativity, innovation, and problem-solving. Of particular interest to StudioLab is its research into the specific roles different shared media perform within design teams. Studying software design teams at Stanford, Grosskopf, Edelman, Steinert, and Leifer write:

> Design Thinking research suggests that each instantiation of media affords particular types of interactions and changes to a designed solution. This happens because the media-model dimensions (abstraction, resolution, ease of change) define the interaction space in which people can define their solution.[30]

---

[30] Alexander Grosskopf, Edelman, Steinert and Leifer. 'Design Thinking implemented in Software Engineering Tools,' 2010, n.p. https://bpt.hpi.uni-potsdam.de/pub/Public/AlexanderGrosskopf/DTRS8_DTinSE.pdf

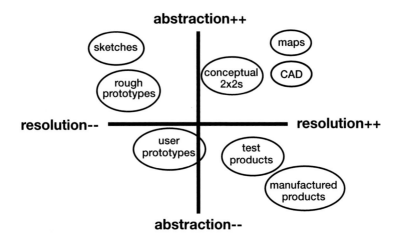

Fig. 4.3 Media models framework, based on Grosskopf et al. (2010)

The authors visualize and correlate these dimensions of different media forms using a conceptual 2 × 2 framework, one composed of two intersecting axes indicating higher and lower levels of resolution (horizontal axis) and abstraction (vertical axis) and arrayed with different media used by software development teams. Low resolution, highly abstract media in the top left quadrant include notes and sketches; high resolution, low abstraction media in the lower right include manufactured products; user prototypes fall near the middle range of both resolution and abstraction (Fig. 4.3).

Significantly, different shared media afford different design changes and different creative moves, ranging from incremental and parametric changes to comprehensive and global ones.

> We call media which affords parametric change analytic media, and media, which affords a multiplicity of potential global solutions generative media. In lab experiments with designers we have observed that analytic media leads people to discuss adjustments of parameters within the design, while generative media affords discussions of the general concept of the design.[31]

---

[31] Alexander Grosskopf et al., 'Design Thinking implemented in Software Engineering Tools,' 2010, n.p. https://bpt.hpi.uni-potsdam.de/pub/Public/AlexanderGrosskopf/DTRS8_DTinSE.pdf

Low res, highly abstract media models (e.g., a small plastic car) are generative media as they open possibilities of global change; high res, very concrete media models (e.g., a fully functional car) are analytic media as they afford narrow parametric change. Big changes happen through generative media, small changes through analytic media.

We can extend these insights about the role of different media in design far beyond software design and connect them to the generation of thought-action figures across different domains: architects, choreographers, engineers, lawyers, urban planners, writers, teachers, students, administrators, all regularly generate projects—each with distinct sets of media forms—that move from fuzzy low res, highly abstract schematics scribbled, typed, or drawn on a surface, toward the iterative creation of sharp, high res, fully concretized things, events, or processes. StudioLab's thought-action figures emerge across these transmedia iterations, with evolving edges of abstraction/concreteness and sharpness/fuzziness. Perhaps all processes, all art, science, education, and even nature and culture can be seen as dynamic events of transmedia figuration, with or without ideation.

Design thinking enables StudioLab's critical design teams to work with community partners to identify and enhance the transmedia knowledge at work in processes important to them, while at the same time addressing Mission 3, the transvaluation of performative values. What challenges, dreams, and projects are potential partners grappling with as a community? Where might transvaluations of cultural, technological, and organizational performance occur, and through what media forms are community desires best articulated?

We can map the 3Ps into the interactive dimensions of shared media using the HCD staging of design thinking. *The movement from generative media to analytic media traces the general movement of design thinking as well as performative transvaluation*: low res, abstract media enable teams to *hear* and respond to human desirability and cultural efficacy; rough and ready prototypes probing technical feasibility and technological effectiveness enable them to *create* possibilities; and high res, concrete media models test financial viability and organizational efficiency in order to *deliver* a teams' critical design solutions. Thinking moves from divergent to convergent, as generative abductive leaps and conductive flashes give way to analytical inductive and deductive steps as the DT process unfolds.

140   J. MCKENZIE

Actions, too, transform: through iterative cycles, the 3Ps move across the media-models framework from upper left to center to lower right: from efficacious performance to effective performance to efficient performance—though once again orchestration best figures just how, when, and why each performance comes to the fore or recedes to the background in the iterative, collaborative, and multivalent process. It is through the combination of transformative thought and action, figures and their performance, that performative transvaluation occurs. Combined with critical thinking and tactical media, design thinking enables critical design teams to produce collective, transformative thought-action. In the field, critical design teams can help partners orchestrate when and where different performances are called for, what patterns of thinking are needed, and what forms of transmedia knowledge can best enable the co-design of shared, emergent worlds.

WHAT COULD BE: PLATO COSMOGRAM

In grappling with Plato's Fight Club, we have generated StudioLab as one such emergent world, and early on we posed it as a heterotopia for creating other heterotopias. We can now figure StudioLab as a cosmogram for generating other cosmograms. Becoming cosmographer means co-designing worlds through community engagement, articulating What Is and imagining What Could Be—and then collaboratively designing and creating worlds through transmedia knowledge and performative transvaluation at whatever scale and duration is appropriate.

Design thinking research provides two final concepts for helping critical design teams co-design these worlds. In his dissertation, *Understanding Radical Breaks: Media and Behavior in Small Teams Engaged in Redesign Scenarios,* Jonathan Edelman analyzes radical breaks that occur 'in the course of a redesign when designers make a major departure from the provided artifact.'[32] Radical breaks introduce global, comprehensive change tied to generative media: in our terms, they constitute radical transmediations. Edelman focuses on the role of objects and worlds in radical breaks, and underneath each are revealing concepts borrowed from child psychologist Alison Gopnik: *counterfactuals* and *paracosms.* Edelman writes:

---

[32] Jonathan Edelman, 'Understanding Radical Breaks: Media and Behavior in Small Teams Engaged in Redesign Scenarios' (Dissertation. Stanford University), http://purl.stanford.edu/ps394dy6131, p. 59.

4 BECOMING COSMOGRAPHER: CO-DESIGNING WORLDS   141

New solutions are, needless to say, 'counterfactuals'; they stand in contrast to what exists, as exemplified by the object to be redesigned. The 'world' in which they arise can be seen as a 'paracosmos'; generated by design engineers to justify, support, and develop new ideas. The extent to which the paracosmos is unpacked or developed often determines the refinement of the idea.[33]

In play, children create imaginary friends and worlds; in design, teams create counterfactuals and paracosms. Gopnik defines the term 'paracosm' in her book, *The Philosophical Baby: What Children's Minds Tell Us About Truth, Love, and the Meaning of Life*, to discuss the made-up worlds of children and their relation to other life worlds. '"Paracosms" are imaginary societies, rather than imaginary people. They are invented universes with distinctive languages, geography, and history. The Brontës invented several paracosms when they were children.'[34] For Gopnik, paracosms help us think about possible worlds, 'what we call dreams and plans, fictions and hypotheses. They are products of hope and imagination. Philosophers, more drily, call them "counterfactuals."'[35] Paracosms are possible worlds, as are theory and theater. As cosmographers, critical design teams help communities concretize their dreams and plans through the design of counterfactual paracosms with the potential of actualization via transmedia knowledge production.

As cosmogram, StudioLab offers the liberal arts an evolving pedagogic prototype, one transmediated at different sites with different students, faculty, and community partners. Decades old, its design frames tried and tested, the pedagogy remains emergent and offers different possible worlds for others interested in co-designing still other possible worlds through transmedia knowledge and performative transvaluation. In this latest iteration, StudioLab becomes a paracosm for generating paracosms. Its invented multiverse can be mapped by replaying and rearticulating the three missions that issue its call to adventure and guide its call to action.

Mission 1: *Democratize digitality.* The call to adventure here involves a different image of knowledge, a transmedia knowledge composed of thought-action figures that mix ideas and images, logic and stories,

---

[33] Ibid.
[34] Alison Gopnik, *The Philosophical Baby: What Children's Minds Tell Us About Truth, Love, and the Meaning of Life* (New York: Farrar, Straus and Giroux, 2009) 53–54.
[35] Ibid., 19.

142   J. MCKENZIE

episteme and *doxa*. At a deeper level, transmedia knowledge incarnates digitality, an emerging onto-historical apparatus whose modes of subject formation, social organization, and technical infrastructure mixes the apparatuses of Platonic literacy and Homeric orality. StudioLab seeks to democratize digitality just as nineteenth-century educators sought to democratize literacy. The call to action here: *become maker* of transmedia knowledge, use the CAT frame to explore the conceptual, aesthetic, and technical dimensions of thought-action figures by combining learning activities found in seminar, studio, and lab spaces.

Mission 2: *Democratize design.* This call for adventure seeks a different mode of thinking and acting, shifting both critical and creative processes from the model of the lone original genius to that of recombinant collaborators. Connecting critical thinking to tactical media-making, the subversive energies of all-too-Romantic bachelor machines become reorganized into critical design teams, small desiring-machines or intimate bureaucracies modeled on activist cells, garage bands, and start-ups. The call to action here: *become builder* of shared experiences and collaborative platforms, use the UX frame to enable scalability and sustainability of transmedia knowledge production for different stakeholders by connecting with their experiential architectures, their ways of designing worlds.

Mission 3: *Remix performative values.* This call for adventure entails entering the fourth space of thinking and acting, the community field where transmedia knowledge becomes civic discourse and expert knowledge finds new grounds in common knowledge and participatory research. Collaborating with community partners, critical design teams use transmedia knowledge to address local needs and desires and explore how values of cultural efficacy, technical effectiveness, and organizational efficiency shape partners' experiences of the world. The call to action here: *become cosmographer* or co-designer of worlds, use the design-thinking frame to collaboratively attune human desirability, technical feasibility, and financial viability by orchestrating performances and actualizing imagined worlds.

If Plato's Fight Club has understood the world through literacy and ideas, StudioLab seeks to help co-design it through digitality and collective thought-action figures. Plato constitutes one such figure and his Academy forms an experiential architecture reborn over the last two centuries as a global network of modern universities. On this plateau of a

4 BECOMING COSMOGRAPHER: CO-DESIGNING WORLDS

Fig. 4.4 Still from "Plato in Play-Dough," YouTube video, 2012, Sophie Klomparens, Caleb Klomparens, and Calvin Klomparens

thousand dancing Platos, we now find a philosophical child, one playing with factual and counterfactual family and friends as they transform a Google School project into a 3D paracosm. With her hands she models small colorful forms of Plato, Socrates, Meletos, Menon, Criton, and Antyos, figures they will use in a thought-action animation depicting the trial and death of Socrates. It is a primal scene of community engagement. Via transmedia knowledge, other worlds emerge (Fig. 4.4).

References

An Introduction to Design Thinking: Process Guide. 2019. Hasso Plattner Institute of Design, Stanford University. https://dschool-old.stanford.edu/sandbox/groups/designresources/wiki/36873/attachments/74b3d/ModeGuideBOOTCAMP2010L.pdf. Accessed 12 Jan 2019.

Anderson, Frank, Beverly Bickel, Lee Boot, Sherella Cupid, Denise Griffin Johnson, and Christopher Kojzar. n.d. The Art of Transformation: Cultural Organizing by Reinventing Media. *Public* 4: 2. http://public.imaginingamerica.org/blog/article/the-art-of-transformation-cultural-organizing-by-reinventing-media/. Accessed 10 Feb 2019.

Austin, J.L. 1962. *How to Do Things With Words: The William James Lectures*. London: Oxford University Press. SBN-13: 978-0674411524.

144 J. MCKENZIE

Birch, June, Lia Ruttan, Tracy Muth, and Lola Baydala. 2009. Culturally Competent Care for Aboriginal Women: A Case for Culturally Competent Care for Aboriginal Women Giving Birth in Hospital Settings. *International Journal of Indigenous Health* 4 (2): 24–34.

Brown, Tim. 2009. *Change by Design: How Design Thinking Transforms Organizations and Inspires Innovation*. New York: Harper Collins.

De Vuono-powell, Saneta, Chris Schweidler, Alicia Walters, and Azadeh Zohrabi. 2015. *Who Pays? The True Cost of Incarceration on Families*. Oakland: Ella Baker Center, Forward Together, Research Action Design.

Edelman, Jonathan. 2011. *Understanding Radical Breaks: Media and Behavior in Small Teams Engaged in Redesign Scenarios*. Dissertation, Stanford University. http://purl.stanford.edu/ps394dy6131

Frank, David, and Michelle Bolduc. 2004. From *vita contemplativa* to *vita activa*: Chaïm Perelman and Lucie Olbrechts-Tyteca's Rhetorical Turn. In *Advances in the History of Rhetoric*, ed. Robert N. Gaines, vol. 7, 65–86.

Gardner, Lee. 2017a. Can Design Thinking Redesign Higher Ed? *The Chronicle of Higher Education*, September 10. www.chronicle.com/article/Can-Design-Thinking-Redesign/241126. Accessed 7 July 2018.

———. 2017b. How Design Thinking Can Be Applied Across the Campus. *The Chronicle of Higher Education*, September 10. www.chronicle.com/article/How-Design-Thinking-Can-Be/241127. Accessed 7 July 2018.

Gopnik, Alison. 2009. *The Philosophical Baby: What Children's Minds Tell Us About Truth, Love, and the Meaning of Life*. New York: Farrar, Straus and Giroux.

Grosskopf, Alexander, Jonathan Edelman, Martin Steinert, and Larry Leifer. 2010. Design Thinking Implemented in Software Engineering Tools: Proposing and Applying the Design Thinking Transformation Framework. https://bpt.hpi.uni-potsdam.de/pub/Public/AlexanderGrosskopf/DTRS8_DTinSE.pdf

Hopkins, Zoe, and Amancay Nahuelpan. 2012. *It Takes a Village*, ed. Sean Muir. The Healthy Aboriginal Network.

IDEO. 2009. *Human-Centered Design Toolkit*. https://www.ideo.com/work/human-centered-design-toolkit/

Kimbell, Lucy. 2011. Rethinking Design Thinking, Part 1. *Design and Culture* 3 (3): 285–306. https://doi.org/10.2752/175470811X13071166525216.

Klomparens, Sophie, Caleb Klomparens, and Calvin Klomparens. 2012. Plato with Play-Dough. YouTube video, May 28. https://www.youtube.com/watch?v=_GH3CRMLskQ. Accessed 11 Feb 2019.

MacKenzie, Donald A. 2006. *An Engine Not a Camera: How Financial Models Shape Markets*. Cambridge, MA: MIT Press.

Mangum, Teresa. 2017. Welcome to Digital Engagements; Or, the Virtual Gets Real. *Public* 4 (2). http://public.imaginingamerica.org/blog/issues/digital-engagements-when-the-virtual-gets-real/. Accessed 10 Feb 2019.

Mayer, Ralo. 2006. *How to Do Things With Worlds 1*. Innsbruck: Künstlerhaus Büchsenhausen.

Miller, Peter N. 2015. Is Design Thinking the New Liberal Arts? *The Chronicle of Higher Education*, March 26. https://www.chronicle.com/article/Is-Design-Thinking-the-New/228779. Accessed 15 Feb 2016.

The Design Thinking Initiative. n.d. The Design Thinking Initiative. Smith College. Retrieved May 15, 2016, from http://smith.edu/design-thinking/

Turner, Victor. 1974. Liminal to Liminoid, in Play, Flow, and Ritual: An Essay in Comparative Symbology. *Rice Institute Pamphlet – Rice University Studies* 60 (3). Rice University.

Warmath, Dee. Redesigning the Process of Carrying Stuff. Unpublished Worksheet.

Index[1]

A
Alan Alda Centre for Communicating Science, 39–42
Alphabetic writing
  as audiovisual medium, ix, 10
  and critical thinking, ix, 6, 18, 30
  and Platonism, 3
Antonin, Artaud, 9, 60, 104
Aristotle
  poetics, 10, 93
Art activism, 6, 24, 85
Art of Transformation (AoT)
  cultural organizing, 121–123

B
Bands, viii, 17, 30, 71, 73, 75, 86–89, 92, 98, 101, 110, 125, 142
Bateson, Gregory
  plateau of intensity, 72
Becoming

becoming builder, 30, 70–105, 110, 112
becoming cosmographer, 30, 102, 110–143
becoming maker, 30, 34–65, 102, 103, 110, 112
  as flow, 101
  as plateau of intensity, 72
  as transformation, 23, 30, 70, 110
Brecht, Bertolt, 60, 93
Bricoleurs, 70, 110
Brown, Tim, 17, 127, 128, 135, 136
Builders, 13–15, 19–21, 30, 31, 65, 70–105

C
Cage, John
  Fluxus, 52, 53, 97
  4.33, 52
  silence, 52, 57, 96–98

---

[1] Note: Page numbers followed by 'n' refer to notes.

© The Author(s) 2019
J. McKenzie, *Transmedia Knowledge for Liberal Arts and Community Engagement*, Digital Education and Learning, https://Doi.org/10.1007/978-3-030-20574-4

147

148 INDEX

CAT (Conceptual-Aesthetic-Technical) frame
CATO, 98, 100
sleepy CATs, 56–60
Co-consulting
as world building, 133–135
Co-designing worlds, 110–143
Cold War
ARPANET, 7
unwinding of funding, 7
Collaboration, *see* Critical design teams
Collaborative analytics, 122, 126
Collaborative platforms, ix, 13, 14, 23, 30, 70–105, 110, 122–124, 126, 134, 135, 142
See also Experiential architectures
Collective thought-action, x, 24, 71, 100–105, 142
See also Thought-action figures
Community engagement
broader impacts, 112
citizen science, 30
collaborative analytics, 122
community partners, 121, 125, 135
community relationships, 121
cultural organizing, 120
participatory research, 30
public humanities, 30
Cornell University
Engaged Cornell, xvi
Public Service Center, 126, 133, 134
Cosmograms
as heterotopias, 140
as paracosm, 141
as world building, 140–143
Cosmographers, 13, 19–21, 30, 31, 65, 103, 110–112, 120, 135, 140–142
Creativity
ideational brainstorming in DT, 130
recombinant bricoleur, 110

Romantic genius, 30, 70, 74, 100, 110
See also Becoming
Crisis of the liberal arts, vii, 3, 5–10, 12, 16, 27, 43, 56, 112
Critical Art Ensemble (CAE)
collaboration, 73
tactical media, 17, 21, 73–75
as tutor group, 73
Critical design
Bardzell and Bardzell, 15
as combination of critical thinking, tactical media and design thinking, 26
Dunne and Raby, 15, 35–37
Critical design teams
bands, 17, 30, 101, 125, 142
as desiring-machines, 22, 71–73, 79, 104, 142
guilds, 73, 89, 92, 125
as intimate bureaucracies, 22, 73, 89–90, 103, 142
role-playing, 81, 85, 87, 89, 98, 111, 124, 135
teams, 17–19, 22, 30, 70–73, 76, 79, 81–85, 87–90, 92, 97, 98, 101–105, 110, 111, 124–129, 135, 137, 139–142
Critical management studies (CMS), 19, 20, 125
Critical thinking
and critical design, ix, 5, 16, 17, 19, 26, 28, 30, 34, 36, 37, 45, 53, 64, 71, 79, 103, 110, 127, 140
and critical theory, 5, 16
as Essential Learning Outcomes (ELO), 5, 8, 16
and Platonism, 7
in StudioLab, ix, 5, 14–18, 26, 28, 34, 37, 64, 71, 79
and writing, ix, 5, 13, 28, 34, 49, 53, 64, 71, 110, 127

D

Dance Your PhD, *see* Transmedia knowledge
Deleuze, Gilles
  desiring-machines, 71
  planes of consistency and organization, 104
    Plateau, 104
    rhizomes, 45
Derrida, Jacques
  generalized writing, 11
  of *Grammatology*, 11
  logocentrism as ethnocentrism, 11
  disseminations, 78n12
Descartes, Rene, 7, 13, 16, 39, 70, 77
Design a Museum project, 22
DesignLab
  smart media, 42–44
  as tutor site, 42
Design thinking (DT)
  as design frame, 127–133
  d.school at Stanford, 113–115
  financial viability, 127, 142
  five phases, 128
  human desirability, 18, 24, 31, 90, 103, 127, 128, 142
  IDEO, 113, 127, 136
  as new liberal arts, 113
  technical feasibility, 18, 24, 31, 90, 127, 142
  three spaces, 136
Digitality
  as apparatus, viii, ix, 16, 39, 64, 83, 84, 142
  defined, 14
  as onto-historical formation, viii, 72
Doxa, 2, 9, 18, 26, 35, 43, 44, 53, 56, 58–60, 63, 64, 78, 110, 111, 114, 118, 119, 123, 125, 131, 142
Duarte, Nancy, 60–64, 94, 137

E

Ella Baker Center for Human Rights
  Who Pays?, 118–120
EmerAgency
  as tutor group, 83–86
Enlightenment, 7, 10, 38, 39
Episteme, 2, 9, 18, 26, 35, 43, 44, 56, 58–60, 63, 64, 78, 110, 111, 114, 118, 119, 123, 125, 131, 142
Essential Learning Outcomes (ELO), 5, 6, 8, 16
Experience design, 21–23, 30, 88, 92, 93, 95–98, 101, 102, 110, 131, 133, 137
Experience economy, 91
Experiential architectures, 23, 30, 31, 99–105, 123, 135, 142

F

Flow, 9, 12, 34, 45, 46, 64, 72, 80, 85, 93, 97, 99, 101, 102, 104, 114, 130
Foucault, Michel
  disciplinary power knowledge, 70
  heterotopias, 31

G

Genres
  emerging scholarly genres, x, 42, 43, 98
  traditional scholarly genres, x
Google
  Google Classroom, viii, 79
  googlization, 77–79, 84
  as tutor group, 79
Graphe, 18, 59
Graphic essays, *see* Transmedia knowledge

150 INDEX

Guattari, Felix
  desiring-machines, 71
  planes of consistency and
    organization, 104
  rhizomes, 45
Guerrilla Girls
  art-galleries, 80
  discrimination, 79–81
  feminism, 80, 85
  masks, 47, 79–81, 85
  tactical-media, 79–81
  as tutor group, 82
Guilds, 30, 73, 86–89, 92, 98, 125

H
Havelock, Erik, 9
Homer, 3, 9, 12
Human-centered design, 6, 14, 17,
    21, 58, 59, 111, 115, 118, 119,
    123, 128, 132, 136, 137

I
Ideas (*edios*)
  in collaboration, 21, 73, 124
  in design, 18, 21, 44, 60, 124,
    129–132
  in StudioLab, 6, 9, 24, 36, 38, 44,
    47, 64, 129, 131, 132
Indigenous Story Studio (ISS)
  Healthy Aboriginal Network,
    115, 126
  It Takes a Village, 116–118
  Muir, Sean, 115–116, 118
  as tutor group, 115–118
Info comics, *see* Transmedia
  knowledge
Information architecture, *see* UX
  (User Experience) frame
Information design, *see* UX
  (User Experience) frame

Interdisciplinarity
  in collaboration, 3
  in design, 18, 21
Intimate bureaucracy, 22, 23, 73,
    89–90, 98, 100–104, 115, 142

L
Learning spaces
  field, 31, 110, 123, 129
  labs, 31, 70, 86, 88, 110, 123,
    125, 142
  media studios, 37
  seminars, 31, 70, 86, 110, 123, 142
  studios, 31, 70, 86, 88, 110, 123,
    129, 142
  See also Collaborative platforms
LeFever, Lee, 58, 59, 63, 64, 137
Literacy, viii, ix, 9, 14–16, 39, 46, 47,
    56, 64, 65, 77–79, 84–86, 115,
    134, 142
Logic (*logos*)
  abductive, 74
  conductive, 74, 84
  deductive, 74, 84
  inductive, 74
Lyotard, Jean-Francois, 7, 8, 19,
    46, 63
  performativity of postmodern
    knowledge and social bonds, 125

M
Makers, 8, 12–15, 19, 28, 30, 31, 34,
    35, 44, 46, 53, 56–59, 64, 70,
    72, 73, 86, 89, 103, 105, 114,
    116, 123, 135
  becoming maker, 30, 34–65, 102,
    103, 110, 112, 142
Media
  alphabetic writing, 12, 13, 29,
    30, 123

INDEX   151

analytic media, 138, 139
audiovisual media, ix, 10, 29
digital media, ix, 5, 6, 12, 13, 26,
    34, 35, 37, 43, 47, 48, 73, 83,
    93, 120–121, 134
generative media, 138–140
media cascades, 46–48
media-forms framework, 28, 49,
    125, 138
monomedia, 4, 12, 28
multimedia, ix, x, 12–14, 26, 29,
    42–44, 47, 61, 72, 73, 87
shared media in DT, 24, 103
tactical media, ix, 6, 16–18, 20–24,
    26, 30, 31, 37, 71, 73–75,
    79–82, 86, 102, 110, 127,
    140, 142
transmedia, viii, 4, 34–65, 71, 110
Mythos, 2, 9, 26, 38, 39, 59, 60

O
Orality, 9, 15, 39, 78, 79, 85, 142

P
PechaKucha, *see* Transmedia
    knowledge
Performances
    cultural, 19–21, 73, 135, 139
    orchestration of, 137–143
    organizational, 19–21, 73, 98–100,
        135, 139
    technological, 19–21, 73, 135, 139
Performativity
    Butlerian, 126
    critical performativity, 19, 20, 126
    cultural efficacy, 8, 18, 21, 24, 31,
        126, 128
    Lyotardian, 125
    organizational efficiency, 8, 18, 21,
        24, 31, 126, 128

remix of performative values, 21,
    31, 115, 126, 142
technological effectiveness, 8, 21
transvaluation of performative
    values, 31, 100, 126, 139
Pharmakon, 47, 65n30, 78, 79
Plato
    academy, 2, 3, 6, 10, 31, 64, 65,
        103, 104, 142
    Epinomis, 65n30
    Phaedrus, 59, 78n12
    Plato's Fight Club, 2–31, 42, 64, 70,
        96, 97, 103, 110, 114, 140, 142
    The Republic, 3, 10, 42, 65, 77
Post-ideational thinking, 6, 43, 45, 86
    post-Platonic thought, 15, 18, 112,
        114, 131

R
Rainer, Yvonne, 48

S
Shared experiences, 14, 23, 30, 39,
    57, 58, 70, 71, 73, 100, 101,
    110, 123, 125, 126, 134,
    135, 142
    See also Experiential architectures
Sparklines, 60–64, 61n28, 94, 137
StoryCentre
    as tutor site, 37, 123
Students
    as builders, 14, 19, 70, 86, 87,
        89, 112
    as cosmographers, 13, 111, 135
    as makers, 12, 13, 19, 30, 35, 44
StudioLab
    as critical design pedagogy, 14–18,
        21, 24, 26, 28, 31, 36, 127
    as transversal pedagogy across
        learning phases, 22

152 INDEX

T
TED talks, *see* Transmedia knowledge
Thinking
  convergent, 130–132, 139
  divergent, 130, 139
  figural, viii, 46
  ideational, viii, 13, 16
Thought-action figures
  in contrast to ideas, 113, 141
  examples of, 130, 135
  and media cascades, 46–48
  as new image of thought, viii,
    46, 64
Transmedia knowledge
  academic articles, 11, 28, 44, 98
  conference presentations, x, 57, 93
  Dance Your PhD, 40, 42, 44, 47
  graphic essays, 43, 50, 87, 100
  info comics, x, 44, 124
  installations, x, 60, 74
  lecture performances, 44
  as mix of *episteme* and *doxa*, 44, 53,
    60, 78
  PechaKuchas, 124
  posters, x, 28, 29, 42, 48, 60, 74,
    111, 124
  science rap, 44, 47
  TED talks, x, 42, 48
  videos, 28, 43, 48, 74, 91, 97,
    115, 124

  vlogs, 42
  websites, 12, 26, 29, 35, 43, 74, 91,
    100, 120

U
Ulmer, Gregory L.
  conduction, 74
  cosmogram, 117
  electracy, viii, 84
  konsultancy (*see* EmerAgency)
UX (User Experience) frame
  experience design, 23, 30, 92, 96,
    98, 101, 102, 110
  information architecture, 23, 30,
    95, 98, 110
  information design, 23, 30, 94,
    95, 98

V
Vlogs, *see* Transmedia knowledge

W
Wagstaff, Steel, xv, 50–53, 50n25,
  57, 96, 97
Why, What, and How, 56–60, 64,
  125, 137
Writing, *see* Alphabetic writing; Media